THE PHILOSOPHY OF GANDHI

THE

PHILOSOPHY OF GANDHI

A study of his basic ideas

GLYN RICHARDS

CURZON PRESS
BARNES & NOBLE BOOKS

First published 1982
Reprinted 1983

Curzon Press Ltd: London and Dublin
and
Barnes & Noble Books: Totowa, NJ, USA

ISBN
UK 0 7007 0150 8
US 0 389 20247 9

Library of Congress Cataloging in Publication Data

Richards, Glyn.
        The philosophy of Gandhi.

        Bibliography: p.
        Includes index.
        1. Gandhi, Mahatma, 1869-1948. I. Title.
B133.G4R52 1982   181'.4   81-14859
ISBN 0-389-20247-9   AACR2

Printed and bound in Great Britain by
Biddles Ltd, Guildford and King's Lynn

To Helga

CONTENTS

PREFACE

I wish to express my thanks and indebtedness to the following for sharing with me their recollections of Gandhi: Morarji Desai, who despite the pressures and demands of his office as Prime Minister, spared the time to answer my questions and make some valuable suggestions; Nayar Pyarelal, who in his enthusiasm for the subject gave unstintingly of his time and knowledge; and Ācārya J. B. Kripalani, who submitted to my constant questioning with patience and grace and who provided me with many valuable insights.

I am indebted also to Prabhudas Balubhai Patwari, Governor of Tamil Nadu, whose gracious hospitality made the meeting with Ācārya Kripalani possible; Professors R. R. Verma and her colleagues of Lucknow University; Margaret Chatterji, Delhi University; N. S. Dravid and his colleagues of Nagpur University; V. A. Devasenapathi, Madras University; and D. P. Chattopadhyay, Jadvapur University, for their readiness to discuss Indian philosophical issues with me; Professors Russell Chandran and F. Muliyhill of the United Theological College, Bangalore, for giving me an Indian Christian perspective on Gandhi's thought; Professors John E. Smith and Norvin Heim of Yale University for some valuable suggestions; and Professors L. M. Read and Nalini Devdas of Carleton University, Ottawa, and D. Z. Phillips of the University College, Swansea, for reading the manuscript and for their pertinent criticisms and comments.

Finally a word of appreciation is due to the University of Stirling for making it possible for me to do the research necessary for this book; to my colleagues Antony Duff and Sandra Marshall for their comments and suggestions; and to Shona Muir and Davina Campbell for typing the manuscript.

GLYN RICHARDS

CHAPTER I

THE CONCEPT OF TRUTH

The concept of Truth (Satya) is fundamental to the thought of Gandhi. It is not without significance that the sub-title of his autobiography is 'The Story of my experiments with Truth', and his whole life might well be interpreted as an attempt to live in accordance with or an existential quest for Truth. Followers of Gandhi explicitly maintain that he was essentially a practical man with no concern for metaphysics or philosophical speculation, yet it is clear that whenever he attempted to explain what he meant by Truth he was involved in metaphysical speculation whether he or his followers realized it or not. My contention is that the unity of Gandhi's thought and the interrelatedness of the various aspects of his teaching spring from firmly-held metaphysical beliefs and that the nature of these beliefs become very much apparent when he expounds what he means by Truth. I am not suggesting that he arrives at the meaning of Truth as the result of philosophical or metaphysical speculation in a vacuum. He is not a neutral observer who first learns to define Truth and then applies it to different aspects of life. Rather he is a participant in a form of life and the meaning of Truth for him is made apparent from the way in which it is used in that form of life.

Gandhi is faithful to the traditions of Hinduism when he affirms the isomorphism of Truth (Satya) and Reality (Sat). He refers to reality as Truth and by the use of the term he preserves the metaphysical and ethical connotation of such traditional Hindu terms as dharma, universal law or duty, and ṛta, the cosmic moral law. For him nothing is, or nothing exists, except Truth,[1] and where Truth is there also is true knowledge, (cit), and where true knowledge is, there also is bliss, (ānanda). Truth then is Saccidānanda, being, consciousness, bliss. This may be one of the reasons why Gandhi has no difficulty in describing himself as an Advaitin or non-Dualist,[2] though to what extent it is accurate to regard Gandhi as an Advaitin is another matter. It is evident that he has no difficulty either in describing himself as a Dvaitin or Dualist, or as a follower of Viśiṣṭādvaita or qualified non-Dualism, namely, non-Dualism with distinctions. But his claim to be able to represent the three major philosophical schools of the Vedānta does not prevent him from regarding Truth (Satya) as the most correct and most fully significant term that could be used for God. On the face of it the statement 'God is Truth' seems to imply that Truth is an attribute or description of God, and in the first instance Gandhi was content to allow the phrase to be used in this way although it did not accurately reflect his position. Later, however, he came to realize that it was more accurate for him to say Truth is God than it was to say God is Truth. That is, he considered the term God to be an appellation for Truth rather than the term Truth to be a description or attribute of God. The statement 'Truth is God', which Gandhi instinctively felt to be a more accurate expression of his basic position, is not inconsistent with his description of Truth as Being itself, as eternal, or with his reference to Truth as that which alone is, all else being momentary. While in his view Truth need not assume shape or form at any time, yet when it is made to do so in order to meet specific human needs it is called Īśvara or God and assumes a personal connotation.[3]

For Gandhi, however, the primary connotation of the term 'God' is not personal. He describes God as a force, as the essence of life, as pure, undefiled consciousness, as truth, goodness, light and love, and as the atheism of the atheist since the latter also seeks truth. He rejects the suggestion that Buddhism can be considered atheistic on the grounds that God is really the dharma or teaching of the Buddhists.[4] He sees God as the unseen power pervading all things, the sum-total of life, the indefinable, the formless, the nameless. What these descriptions present us with is the concept of an impersonal Absolute or Ultimate and this is exactly what Gandhi wishes to convey for he has no hesitation in expressing a preference for the idea of God as formless Truth.[5] Yet his expressed preference for the worship of the formless does not prevent him from recognizing that God is personal to those who need to feel his presence and embodied to those who desire to experience his touch.[6] In his view it makes no difference whether the devotee conceives of God in personal or in impersonal terms since the one class of devotee is not inferior to the other. His readiness to acknowledge that God is all things to all men enables him to support the Dvaitin or Dualist, and Viśiṣṭādvaitin or qualified non-Dualist positions as well as maintaining his own preference for Advaita or non-Dualism. His acceptance of what he calls 'the doctrine of the manyness of reality',[7] by which he probably means that reality can be conceived of in many different ways, makes it possible for him to approve of the non-creative aspect of God as propounded by the Jains, and the creative aspect of God as propounded by Rāmānuja the foremost exponent of the Viśiṣṭādvaita position. That this tolerant attitude should have resulted in his being called an Anekāntavādin, or a believer in many doctriness, is not surprising. but it did not disturb him in the least.[8] His position is such, however, that it does produce the paradox that God is described in the same context as an impersonal force and the essence of life. and also as omniscient, omnipotent, and benevolent.[9] Gandhi moves from impersonal to personal descriptions of God without difficulty and while he expresses preference for an impersonal God he is not averse to describing God in personal terms. This might be interpreted as an indication that it is not his purpose or intention to present a systematic, coherent and consistent Advaitin account of the concept of Truth or God after the fashion of Śankara, the principal exponent of non-dualism, and that what could be said concerning the metaphysical basis of his thought is that although it purports to be Advaitin it does not preclude the possibility of Dvaita, or Dualist, and Viśiṣṭādvaita, or qualified non-Dualist interpretations of the nature of reality. On the other hand, it might be argued that when he moves from the concept of impersonal truth to the concept of a personal God, he is distinguishing, in traditional Advaitin fashion, between higher and lower levels of truth or reality. But acceptance of this argument involves acceptance of the superiority of the higher, impersonal level of truth over the lower personal level of truth and the acknowledgment of two levels of knowledge. Gandhi, as we have seen, sees no superiority in conceiving of God in impersonal rather than personal terms so it is difficult to see how the traditional distinction between higher and lower levels of truth can be applied to him. The fact that he uses both personal and impersonal descriptions of God supports this point. If the question is asked whether Gandhi is not aware of the dangers of contradiction in his use of personal and impersonal terms to describe God, the answer might be that it would depend whether the personal use of the term God refers to an entity, or being, in the form of an extra-mundane person, whether or not a contradiction is involved. Gandhi, however, does not conceive of God in this way even when he uses the term in a personal sense. He insists that 'you labour under a limitation when you think of a being or entity who is beyond the power of a man to grasp',[10] so it can be maintained that he is aware of the problems involved in his personal-impersonal uses of the term God. It might also be maintained that the elasticity of the concept of Satya in Indian philosophical thought may well account for these apparent contradictions.

The foregoing argument may be supported by what Gandhi says about the names and forms of God. He is able to refer to God by such names as Rāma and Kṛṣṇa, which are specifically Hindu names, and as Ahuramazda, which is the Zoroastrian name for the God of light. These names have a personal connotation and, according to Gandhi, are simply man's attempt to define the mysterious, invincible force that pervades all things. In his youth he was taught, in accordance with Hindu custom, to repeat the thousand names of God, but he realized that the thousand names of God were not exhaustive and that while God has many names and many forms he is also nameless and formless.[11] In fact the power that is called God is beyond definition; it is, as is stated of Brahman, 'neti, neti,—not this, not this', and in our attempts to define it we are seeking to describe the indescribable. According to Gandhi, if it is at all possible for man to describe this power then it ought to be called Truth (Satya), which is a derivative of Sat, which literally means that which is or exists. All the names and forms attributed to this indefinable power are, in Gandhi's view, symbols, and attempts to personalize God. Some clearly feel the need for the Ultimate to be expressed in symbolic, personalized form, and image worship can be regarded as part of the desire of human nature for symbols.[12] Personifications of the Ultimate in such forms as Rāma and Kṛṣṇa have to be regarded as symbols which manifest man's craving for the Unseen for what suits one man does not necessarily meet the needs of another.

'I have accepted all the names and forms attributed to God, as symbols connoting one formless omnipresent Rama. To me, therefore, Rama... is the all-powerful essence whose name, inscribed in the heart, removes all suffering, mental, moral and physical.'[13]

When it was suggested to Gandhi on one occasion by a Roman Catholic priest that if Hinduism became monotheistic Christianity and Hinduism could serve India in co-operation, Gandhi's reply was that Hindus were not polytheistic. While it is undoubtedly true that Hindus say there are many gods they also declare that there is but one God, Īśwara, Devādhideva, who is God of gods. Gandhi himself professed to be a thorough Hindu yet not a believer in many gods.[14]

If it is insisted that image worship is nothing but a form of idol worship, Gandhi's response to this accusation is that image worship is simply indicative of man's need for symbols. Hindus do not worship their images of stone or metal. They worship rather God as symbolized or personified in those forms. If a worshipper were to make a fetish of his stone or metal image, however, then that might correctly be construed as idolatry, but such an attitude has to be distinguished from the element of sacredness that worshippers often attribute to temples, churches and mosques or to books such as the Bible, the Koran or the Gītā. Gandhi illustrates his rejection of the charge of idolatry by stating: 'Every Hindu child knows that the stone in the famous temple in Banaras is not Kashi Vishwanath. But he believes that the Lord of the Universe does reside specially in that stone.'[15]

The stone referred to here is clearly a symbol of God rather than an embodiment of God, but at the same time it has an element of sacredness, which is what Gandhi may be implying when he maintains that God resides in the stone in a special way. Or to put it in another way, for Gandhi the stone partakes of the nature of that which it represents.

By the use of the last phrase I have indicated a comparison that may possibly be drawn between Gandhi and Paul Tillich. Gandhi's teaching concerning the symbolic nature of personifications of Truth in a variety of different forms seems on the face of it to correspond to what Tillich has to say about the symbolic nature of Christian terminology. Both maintain that there are symbolic representations of the Ultimate whether the Ultimate be depicted as Truth or as the Holy. For Gandhi, symbols manifest man's craving for the unseen and intangible; for Tillich they are necessary because the Ultimate or Holy could not maintain its unconditional character without them. The difference between the practical approach of Gandhi and the more systematic, theological approach of Tillich is evident from these descriptions. Tillich holds that symbols in themselves cannot be equated with the Ultimate nor can they be regarded as fully expressing the Ultimate. He refers to symbols as pointing beyond themselves to the Ultimate while at the same time partaking of the nature of that to which they point. By this he means that they possess a certain sacred connotation or depth dimension. They open up levels of reality not easily accessible to the more literal approach and relate to elements within the depth of man's soul. Symbols, for Tillich, do not wholly contain the Ultimate and, in his view, there can be no finite particularization of the Ultimate or Holy. To maintain that the Ultimate can be fully expressed in finite particulars can only result in what Tillich calls the demonization of the Holy. Symbols, according to Gandhi, are a necessity for the religious life of some people but he insists that there is nothing inferior in conceiving of God in personalized terms. Furthermore, different religions may need different symbols, and it is only when they are treated as fetishes, or when they become the means whereby one religion claims superiority over another, that they cease to be of value and are fit only to be discarded. In other words, while Tillich maintains that when finite particulars are given the status

of ultimacy it is detrimental to true religion and a form of demonization, Gandhi insists that symbols which become fetishes are
idolatrous and fit only to be discarded. Presumably what he means
is that at that point they will have lost their representative character
and become embodiments of the divine. Tillich would call this
practice demonization, or the elevation of a finite particular to the
status of ultimacy. Gandhi would regard it as a failure to preserve
or maintain the function of symbols and a degeneration of their
purpose. Tillich's tendency to hypostasize the Ultimate in the concept of Ground of Being does not appear to be shared by Gandhi.
True he expresses a preference for the impersonal concept of Truth
(Satya), which etymologically is a derivative of Being (Sat), in con-
templating the Ultimate, but this does not preclude other more personal concepts of God. The reason he gives for adopting this standpoint is that reality can be conceived of in many different ways all
of which are equally valid. It follows that Gandhi's view of symbols
differs somewhat from that of Tillich in the sense that they do not
point to a hypostasized Ultimate. For the latter, the term God is the
main religious symbol for the Ground of Being while, for the former, God is the name we give to the mysterious power that pervades
the universe and not a symbol in the Tillichian sense. The manifestation of God in the Indian tradition would take such forms as
Brahma, Viṣṇu and Śiva, the trimūrti of the Hindu way of life, and
innumerable other gods and goddesses, the veneration of which,
in Gandi's view, is sometimes inaccurately and insensitively described as idol worship. According to Tillich, the way in which God is
filled out with concrete symbols in the Christian tradition is by the
use of certain aspects of man's finite experience. For example, he is
referred to as Father, as Person, as One who acts and who shows
love, power and justice. The essence of idolatry for Tillich is when
these concrete, finite symbols are accorded the status of the Holy
or Ultimate Concern; this is the demonization of religion. According to Gandhi, it is when symbols become fetishes and embodiments
of the divine, that they might be construed as idols. At that point
they cease to serve their purpose and then are fit only to be discarded.[16]

Gandhi claims to be simply a seeker after Truth, ceaselessly searching for it, occasionally having glimpses of it, yet not finding it.[17] It is as if he glimpses absolute Truth in and through particular instances of truth. He does not equate absolute Truth with particular instances of truth but that does not prevent him from recognizing that particular instances of truth, while not embodying absolute Truth, are nevertheless necessary to convey the meaning of absolute Truth. His existential quest for Truth is in fact the key to his understanding and interpretation of the Bhagavad-Gītā. He sees the main aim of the Gītā as a call to action. But since, according to Hindu teaching, actions of themselves bind man to the empirical, saṁsāric world, the endless cycle of birth, death and rebirth, there is need of disciplined action or desireless action, that is, action where there is no hankering after the fruits of action, if liberation is to be achieved. Gandhi would describe such action as selfless, detached, sacrificial and non-violent. It is, in his view, action on behalf of others or action in the service of others. This is the kind of action, he maintains, that results from devotion to Truth, but it is also the means whereby one is enabled to see Truth more clearly. This two-way movement is illustrated by the relation Gandhi envisages between ahiṁsā, or non-violence, and Truth.

'Ahimsa is my God, and Truth is my God. When I look for Ahimsa, Truth says, "Find it through me". When I look for Truth, Ahimsa says "Find it through me".'[18] It is Gandhi's contention that the only inevitable means for the attainment of Truth is ahiṁsā. Ahiṁsā is the means and Truth the end. But since ends and means are convertible terms for Gandhi, Truth and ahiṁsā are intertwined. The practice of ahiṁsā inevitably leads to Truth. Conversely, the practice of hiṁsā can never lead to Truth. What Gandhi may be indicating by this reference to the convertibility of the terms means and ends in his thought is that our religious and ethical ideals not only inform the ends we aim at and endeavour to attain, but also the means we employ to reach them. What could be said is that the same moral demands apply to the means as to the ends in the quest for Truth, and that often difficulties arise because of these demands. That is, ethical or moral considerations 'impose a limit on our purposes and their execution which the distinction between means and ends cannot account for, since means and ends alike come under moral scrutiny'.[19]

I will deal with the problems involved in regarding the way of non-violence as an absolute rule, or infallible guide to conduct, or as the right way in all circumstances without exception, in a later chapter on ahiṁsā. It is sufficient at this stage to point out that there are difficulties in making the categorical statement that the practice of hiṁsā can never lead to Truth. It takes no account of the moral dilemmas of human life.

The social and political implications of Gandhi's quest for Truth will also be dealt with in later chapters and for the moment we shall confine ourselves to such questions as how he goes about acquiring glimpses of absolute Truth and how he knows that it is absolute Truth he has actually caught a glimpse of.

When asked on one occasion what he considered Truth to be, it would seem that Gandhi interpreted the question as a request for information as to how he came to know Truth. In his reply he defines Truth as 'What the voice within tells you'.[20] It is tempting to interpret this statement as a self-authenticating, subjective principle which Gandhi is able to resort to, namely, the voice of his conscience. But the point is that the inner voice, or the voice of conscience, is not self-authenticating. There are criteria which determine the way in which a man thinks and acts, and in Gandhi's case they are the religious and ethical ideals of his own form of life. And to attribute knowledge of Truth to the voice of conscience in this way, or to the religious and ethical criteria of a particular form of life, inevitably brings Gandhi face to face with the problem of the relativity of truth and with the question whether under the circumstances one is justified in talking about absolute Truth at all. That is, there are criteria which determine the way in which others also think and act which may be completely contrary to those of Gandhi. Gandhi actually recognizes the problem of relativity and acknowledges that what may be truth for one may be untruth for another. His proposed solution to this problem

is that before one claims to speak of his inner voice, or the voice
of conscience, he should recognize his limitations, and discipline
himself to cultivate truthfulness, humility, purity and non-violence
and embrace the twin ideals of poverty and non-possession. Put
in another way the proposal is that a man should seek to know
and fully understand the criteria which determine his thoughts
and actions. Gandhi speaks also of the need for abhyāsa, or
single-minded devotion, and vairāgya, or indifference to worldly
life. He maintains that: 'If you would swim on the bosom of the
ocean of Truth you must reduce yourself to a zero'.[21]

The question is whether this can really be regarded as a solution
to the problem of the relativity of truth. Does not a human cypher
or zero have to be capable of hearing the inner voice and, to the
extent that he does hear it, is he not then a human being with
the defects and failings that one normally associates with a human
being? If so, it follows that his apprehension of Truth will of
necessity be partial and relative and that absolute Truth will be
forever beyond his grasp. Gandhi actually acknowledges this
fact; he is above all a practical idealist. He accepts that it is impossible for mortal man to lay claim to attain, or to possess, perfect
Truth. Similarly, it is not possible for him either to give a hard –
and–fast definition of Truth. As Gandhi points out: 'We can
only visualize it in our imagination. We cannot, through the
instrumentality of this ephemeral body, see face to face Truth
which is eternal. That is why in the last resort one must depend on
faith.'[22]

His reference to faith may explain how it is that he is able to
conceive of the notion of absolute Truth which he calls God.
It is an affirmation of faith. When he says Truth is God he is really
making a confession of faith rather than a statement in the indicative mood. Such a confession of faith requires no external
verification in the same way as statements of fact. So when he
maintains that because we are, Truth or God is, or that God is
the sum total of life, it could be argued that he is not presenting us
with some kind of cosmological argument for the existence of
God and that it is not his purpose to argue from the world to

God. It is his contention rather that there can be no proofs for
God's existence which are acceptable to human reason since God
is beyond reason. He admits that it may be possible to use reason
to a limited extent, but he insists that ultimately the existence of
God defies all proof and has to be based on faith which transcends
reason.[23]. In the tradition of Advaita or non-Dualism he refers to
the soul, (Ātman), and God, (Brahman), as knowers rather than
objects of knowledge and claims that it is not possible for mortal
beings by the use of reason alone to know the knower of knowing.[24]

Perfect or absolute Truth, which is known by faith, is beyond
our empirical grasp which means that we must act in the knowledge
that we are holding on to such truth as we are able to apprehend
in this world.

'That relative truth must, meanwhile, be my beacon, my shield
and buckler... Even my Himalayan blunders have seemed trifling
to me because I have kept strictly to this path... I have gone
forward according to my light. Often in my progress I have had
faint glimpses of the Absolute Truth, God, and daily the conviction is growing on me that He alone is real and all else is unreal.'[25]

Without relative truth to hold on to it could be argued that
absolute Truth, which is a matter of faith, would be nothing but
empty utopianism. The point is that since we have here no abid-
ing city the particular instance of truth cannot be identified with
absolute Truth. Yet it is only through particular instances of
truth that we can come to understand what it might mean to
speak of absolute Truth. So relative truth is necessary to convey
the meaning of absolute Truth which we affirm in faith. Relative
truth, as Gandhi states, is our 'beacon' in the sphere of the empirical. So when he claims to have had glimpses of absolute Truth,
it may be reasonable to assume, not that he has caught a glimpse
of some kind of hypostasized Ultimate or extra-mundane entity,
but rather that through his participation in a particular form of
life he is made aware of the need to live and act in accordance
with certain religious and ethical criteria and is informed by the
spirit of what might be called dharma (law), or ṛta (moral law),
or tao (way) but which he prefers to call Truth (Satya) or God.

In addition to the need for humility, discipline and singleminded devotion in the quest for Truth Gandhi lays stress on prayer. His concept of prayer, however, requires analysis and clarification in view of his expressed preference for an impersonal and formless Absolute. It could be said that to understand what he means by prayer is to understand what he means by talking to God. If we were to insist that prayer involves some form of dialogue then it would presuppose that we already know what is meant by the concept of God. To adopt this kind of approach would be to make the meaningfulness of prayer contingent on the acceptance of a particular concept of God. Such an approach would preclude an understanding of what Gandhi means by talking to God.[26]

Prayer for Gandhi is the essence of religion and the core of a man's life. It requires no words; it is not the repetition of an empty formula. While it can be petitional, in its widest sense it is inward communion, and in both cases it cleanses the heart of passion and produces peace, orderliness, and repose in daily life. It would appear that for Gandhi prayer is a form of meditation, which has as its aim self-purification and knowledge of the Truth. The form of prayer is unimportant; whatever the form its aim is to bring us into communion with the divine. It may be interpreted as a spiritual discipline necessary to preserve our humanity and to promote the service of others. Basically, however, it is a means of self-purification and a call to inward searching. As Gandhi understands it, by means of petitionary prayer man invokes the divinity within himself; he petitions the real, higher Self.[27] But the petitionary aspect of prayer is not as important to Gandhi as the communion aspect. He calls prayer 'a longing of the soul' and 'an admission of one's weakness'. As he explains: 'The Deity does not need my supplication, but I, a very imperfect human being, do need his protection as a child that of its father.'[28] This exceedingly personalistic reference to God is paralleled by an impersonal description of the Deity as Truth when Gandhi states: 'This God whom we seek to realize is Truth. Or to put it in another way Truth is God. This Truth is not merely the truth we are expected to speak. It is That which alone is, which constitutes the stuff of which all things are made, which subsists by virtue of its own power, which is not supported by anything else but supports everything that exists.'[29]

Plato draws a distinction between telling the truth and being a truthful man. The man who tells the truth is not the same as the truthful man. Gandhi distinguishes between speaking the truth and Truth. The Truth, which presumably Plato's truthful man, like Gandhi himself, feels the need to live in accordance with, to abide by, to hold fast to, and to uphold, is that which determines the way in which he lives and the spirit in which he travels.

The personal-impersonal nature of Gandhi's descriptions of God is clearly illustrated here but the point already made earlier can be reiterated, namely, that it is not important to him whether God is conceived of in personal or impersonal terms since neither superiority nor inferiority of expression is implied in either case.

When Gandhi maintains that by means of prayer he invokes the divinity within himself it is evident that he draws no hard-and-fast distinction between the Self or Ātman within and God or Truth. This could be considered consistent with Advaitin teaching concerning the Brahman-Ātman identity, namely, that the Soul within is at one with the essence of the universe. Gandhi in fact does conceive the purpose of life to be to know the Self, which for him is equivalent to realizing God or knowing the Truth. The Self or Ātman, released from the bonds of darkness and ignorance or avidyā, is at one with God, and when this unity is realized by means of prayer, bhakti or devotion is transformed into jñāna or knowledge. According to Ācārya Kripalani the Rāma invoked by Gandhi with his dying breath was not the historical Rāma or the mythological Rāma, but rather the highest Self.[30] Gandhi himself refers to Rāma as the all powerful essence whose name is inscribed in the heart.[31] Hence the formless, omnipresent Rāma in Gandhi's thought is at one with the highest Self which in turn is identical with Truth.

Gandhi's quest for Truth or God involves not only bhakti yoga, that is the discipline of prayer and devotion, but also karma yoga, that is, the discipline of action. This is evidenced not only by his insistence on self-discipline but also by his insistence on the realization of Truth through the service of others, and by means of ahiṁsā. We have already noted that he interprets the Gītā as a call to action and it is not without significance that he has been described as one of the foremost activist theoreticians and as a karmayogin. We can leave for the time being, however, the implications of his activist approach to Truth in order to look again at his concept of Truth as hitherto elucidated.

As we have seen, he claims to have had glimpses only of absolute Truth and we have interpreted this to mean that he is often made aware of the need to live and act in accordance with certain ethical and religious principles and to travel in a certain spirit. But there have been other claims to knowledge of absolute Truth. The majority of Christians, for example, would claim that Jesus Christ is the only begotten Son of God and the fullness of Truth. Muslims on the other hand would consider Truth to be the revelation vouchsafed by Allah to his prophet Muhammad. When divergent truth claims of this kind confront us the question that arises is what independent criterion of truth can be produced to determine which claim to truth is the right one? How do we distinguish between divergent truth claims? An appeal to the Bible could be countered with an appeal to the Koran, and an appeal to the verification of the Christian claim in the lives of believing Christians could be countered with an appeal to the verification of the Muslim claim in the lives of believing Muslims. If it is maintained that there has to be an independent criterion of truth, then the difficulty we are confronted with is determining precisely what that criterion might be. Gandhi's tolerant attitude to religions, which will be dealt with in the following chapter, is an indication that he does not consider any religion to have a monopoly of Truth and that includes Hinduism. Yet it has to be acknowledged that his glimpses of absolute Truth came to him through his understanding of, and his faith in, the specific content or the essential teaching of his own religious tradition despite its imperfections. It was within his own mode of religious discourse that he was made aware of the need to travel in a certain spirit and to think and act in accordance with specific religious and ethical criteria to which he gave the name Truth. That is, he acquired his understanding of Truth as a participant in the Hindu way of life.

NOTES TO CHAPTER I

1 *The Selected Works of Mahatma Gandhi*, (Navajivan Publishing House, Ahmedabad, 1968), Vol. VI, pp. 96-7.
2 M. K. Gandhi, *Truth is God*, (Ahmedabad, 1955), pp. 11, 20.
3 *Selected Works*, Vol. VI, p. 97.
4 Ibid., pp. 100-2; cf. *Truth is God*, p. 25.
5 *Selected Works*, Vol. V, pp. 382; cf. *Truth is God*, p. 32.
6 *Truth is God*, p. 10.
7 Ibid., p. 12.
8 Ibid., p. 11.
9 *Selected Works*, Vol. VI, p. 100.
10 N. K. Bose, *Selections from Gandhi*, (Ahmedabad, 1948), p. 4.
11 M. K. Gandhi, *In Search of the Supreme*, edited by V. B. Khar, (Ahmedabad, 1931), Vol. I, p. 10.
12 *All Men are Brothers*, Krishna Kripalani (Ed.), (Unesco, Paris, 1958), pp. 70, 76; cf. Nirmal Kumar Bose, *Selections from Gandhi*, (Ahmedabad, 1948), pp. 262.
13 *In Search of the Supreme*, Vol. I, p. 214; cf. *Truth is God*, p. 108.
14 *In Search of the Supreme*, Vol. I, pp. 27-8.
15 Ibid., p. 230.
16 *All Men are Brothers*, pp. 59-60; Paul Tillich, *Dynamics of Faith*, (Harper & Row, New York, 1958), pp. 45-48; *Systematic Theology*, (Nisbet, London, 1968), Vol. I, pp. 234-42.
17 *Truth is God*, p. 3.
18 Ibid., p. 4.
19 D. Z. Phillips, *Some Limits to Moral Endeavour*, University College, Swansea, 1971, p. 7.
20 *Truth is God*, p. 15. This has a firm root in the Indian tradition. e. g. Manu enumerates one's own intuition (hrdayena abhyanujnata —approved by one's heart) as one of the four or five authorities on Dharma. cf. *In Search of the Supreme*, Vol. I, p. 12; *All Men are Brothers*, p. 71.
21 *All Men are Brothers*, p. 71.
22 Ibid., p. 75.
23 *All Men are Brothers*, p. 56.
24 *Selected Works*, Vol. V, pp. 350-3; Vol. VI, pp. 109, 114.
25 *Truth is God*, p. 32.
26 cf. D. Z. Phillips, *The Concept of Prayer*, (London, 1965).
27 *Truth is God*, pp. 41-4.
28 *In Search of the Supreme*, Vol. I, pp. 188, 178; cf. M. K. Gandhi, *Prayer*, (Ahmedabad, 1977), p. 73.
29 *In Search of the Supreme*, p. 196.
30 This point was made by Ácārya J. B. Kripalani in a discussion we had at the residence of the Governor of Tamil Nadu, Prabhudas Balubhai Patwari, January, 1978; cf. *In Search of the Supreme*, Vol. I, pp. 196, 214.
31 *In Search of the Supreme*, Vol. I, p. 214.

CHAPTER II

TRUTH AND RELIGION

Gandhi's concept of Religion corresponds to his concept of Truth. Truth transcends all concrete or particular instances of truth yet particular instances of truth are necessary in order to understand what it means to speak of absolute Truth. As Gandhi has glimpses of absolute Truth through instances of relative truth so, it might be said, he has glimpses of Religion through particular historical religions. For what he means by Religion, as he points out, is that which underlies all religions. Religion is not equatable with particular religions: it transcends Hinduism, Christianity, Islam, and all other religions, yet it harmonizes them and gives them reality.[1] It is that which binds man indissolubly to Truth. It is belief in an ordered moral government of the universe. It is that permanent element in human nature which causes the soul to be restless until it realizes itself to be at one with Truth or God.[2]

I have suggested that Truth for Gandhi is that which determines the spirit in which he lives, or the religious and ethical criteria which govern the way in which he thinks and acts. His life-story relates his experiments with Truth, or his attempt to live in accordance with certain religious beliefs which were a part of his Hindu heritage. It is because of the inherited beliefs and practices of the Hindu way of life that he is able to claim to be bound indissolubly to Truth. He learns what it means to talk of Truth through its use in the religious context of Hindu tradition and culture. Similarly, it is as a participant in the Hindu way of life that he understands what it means to talk of Religion; he understands the meaning of the term Religion from its use in his own form of life.

The one, true and perfect Religion Gandhi refers to is beyond predication and not capable of being realized within finite existence. No particular religion can ever embody the perfection of Religion or lay claim to a monopoly of Truth. Yet particular religions, it might be said, are necessary to convey the meaning of Religion in the same way as particular truths are necessary to convey the meaning of Truth. But as particular truths do not embody the fullness of Truth so particular religions do not embody the fullness of Religion.

Gandhi describes religions as human constructs or expressions of that which underlies them and gives them reality. All religions possess truth, but all are to some extent erroneous. The heart of one particular religion is identical with the heart of another religion.

'Even as a tree has a single trunk, but many branches and leaves, so there is one true and perfect Religion, but it becomes many, as it passes through the human medium. The one Religion is beyond all speech.'[3]

The question that arises here is whether Gandhi is referring to an 'essence' or 'primordial element' when he speaks of the heart of one religion being identical with the heart of another religion. If that is the case, then it is possible to draw a comparison between Gandhi's teaching and the teaching of such Western thinkers as Schleiermacher and Tillich. Schleiermacher conceives of religion as pre-existing particular historical manifestations which are grounded in the fundamental unity of religion, an *a priori* condition.[4] The transcendental unity of religion is necessary for the existence of positive, historical religions, which are the concrete, historical expressions of the primordial form, the immediate religious consciousness or 'the sense and taste for the Infinite'. No limited, finite positive form of religion can encapsulate the universality or infinitude of religion. The idea that a single, finite form of religion can be universally valid is inappropriate.[5] But it does not follow that finite forms are superfluous because religion has to find expression in concrete forms, and the plurality of particular religions is necessary for the complete manifestation of religion. According to Schleiermacher, each positive religion contains something of the true nature of religion, and the 'primordial form', the 'essence', or 'transcendental unity' of religion, is comprehended not by deducing it from the common elements of particular religions as a kind of abstraction, but in and through the language and traditions of particular religions. Particular religions are true in so far as they succeed in expressing the primordial form of religion which in turn is comprehended only in the depths of particular religions.[6]

As we have seen, Gandhi recognizes that no single religion can embody the whole truth, and that all particular religions contain errors since they are human constructs or formulations, but does it follow necessarily that when he speaks of Religion underlying all human constructs, or at the heart of all religions, he is referring to an 'essence' or an 'entity' or a 'primordial form' of religion after the fashion of Schleiermacher? To speak of religion as if it is a 'primordial form' or an 'entity' is to hypostasize it. But if religion is beyond speech or predication as Gandhi affirms, can it be hypostasized, or referred to as if it is a referent? The same point applies to Tillich's definition of religion as Ultimate Concern which refers not simply to man's subjective concern, that is, the expression of his Ultimate Concern, but what he is ultimately concerned about, or that which is the source of his concern. The referential nature of Ultimate Concern in Tillich's thought is indicative of his tendency to hypostasize the Ultimate. The similarity between Tillich's position and that of Schleiermacher's is illustrated by the fact that his concept of Ultimate Concern is not far removed from Schleiermacher's 'feeling of absolute dependence' which has both a subjective and objective connotation. The problem with maintaining the existence of a 'primordial element' is determining how to go about isolating such an element and how to determine the relative truth of particular religions by means of this 'primordial element' once it is isolated. There may be some truth in the claim that there are problems in seeking to postulate 'a transcendental ideal of which the historical actualities are a succession of mundane and therefore imperfect, compromised manifestations',[7] and that the term religion is not something 'that can be formulated and externalized into an observable pattern theoretically abstractible from the persons who live it'.[8]

It is possible that when Gandhi speaks of Religion, what he may be referring to is not an 'essence' or a 'primordial element' or a 'transcendental unity', but the faith of men which expresses itself

in a variety of different forms. It is the way in which Truth or God
impinges on or finds expression in the lives of people and as far
as Gandhi is concerned it is through the beliefs and traditions of
the Hindu way of life that he finds himself indissolubly bound to
Truth.

All religions, according to Gandhi, are different roads to the
same goal and it is his contention that there will always be a variety
of religions corresponding to different human temperaments and
environments.[9] He echoes the teaching of the Hindu reformer Vive-
kānanda when he maintains that there are as many religions as there
are individuals, and that even within particular, historical religions
there will be different viewpoints manifesting different facets of
the truth.[10] When he suggests that it is of no consequence or
importance which road one takes provided the goal is attained ultimately, he would seem to be implying that the end justifies the
means. Since this is contrary to his teaching concerning the convertibility of means and ends, it is hardly likely that he would be
unconcerned with the kind of religion a person might profess to
follow. It might well be of concern to him, for example, if the
content of a particular religion proved to be at odds with the ethical
criteria he would associate himself with the concept of Truth. He
considers religion without morality to be inconceivable, and if it
denies any of the virtues we normally associate with morality,
such as, truth, mercy and goodness, it does not deserve to be called
religion. To lose our basis in morality is to cease to be religious,
for religion and morality are inescapably bound up with one another.[11] Gandhi's emphasis on Sarvodaya, the welfare of all, as both
an expression of Truth and a means of realizing Truth bears out
this point. He recognizes the theonomous nature of humanitarian
activity. Through the service of humanity, and by action in the
cause of brotherhood, we are brought to a better understanding
of Truth. To help the helpless and feed the hungry is to see God.[12]
Sarvodaya and Truth are so interrelated in Gandhi's thought that
they are like two sides of a coin. What Gandhi may be suggesting
by the statement that the road one takes is unimportant provided
the goal is achieved is that too much importance can be attached

to particular religions, especially when it might result in exclusivist claims being made on behalf of those religions.

Gandhi rejects outright claims made concerning the superior or inferior status of religions. Different religions may have different symbols but no symbol should become a fetish in order to enable one religion to claim superiority over another. Gandhi is unable to harbour the thought, even secretly, that another man's faith is inferior to his own because of his belief that different faiths are God's creation and thereby equally holy.[13] On these grounds he is able to advocate the open and sincere study of religions other than one's own. He enjoins an attitude of respect and reverence towards all religions since they all contain an element of truth. He rejects as mistaken the notion that the study of other religions might undermine or weaken a believer's faith in his own religion. On the contrary, he maintains that such a study might well lead to the extension of one's regard for one's own religion to other religions, and at the same time, provide a better understanding of one's own faith.[14]

The openness Gandhi shows to the plurality of religious traditions is commendable. It indicates that he is not content to confine himself to the small island of his own tradition and culture and consequently not recognize the significance of the spiritual insights of other religious traditions. His rejection of the right of a religion to claim superiority for itself over other religions underlines his claim that no particular religion can embody what he calls the one, true and perfect Religion. In this respect Gandhi propounds views about particular religions similar to those of Tillich. It is the latter's contention that Ultimate Concern, the holy or unconditional, expresses itself in a variety of forms: in painting, which may have no religious content in the traditional sense; in philosophy, when attempts are made to understand the nature of ultimate reality; in ideologies which might normally be regarded as secular, such as, nationalism, socialism and humanism; and in traditional religions.[15] When Ultimate Concern expresses itself in particular religions, and adherents of those religions regard them as embodiments of the Ultimate then, in Tillich's view, the particular has been elevated to the status of ultimacy. This is referred to as a form of idolatry; it is the particularization or objectification of the Ultimate and consequently a form of demonization.[16] Gandhi, as we have seen, uses different terminology when he speaks of the symbols of religion becoming fetishes which, in his view, are idolatrous and fit only to be discarded.[17] Differences in terminology do not disguise the similarity of views expressed by Tillich and Gandhi on the question of the status of particular religions. Where they might differ, as I have already indicated, is on the meaning they would give to the concept of Religion. For Gandhi, particular religions are necessary to convey what it might mean to speak of the one, true and perfect Religion which is beyond predication and not realized within finite existence. Religion is that ideal by which we live and act which, though not embodied in particular religions since all religions are necessarily imperfect, is nevertheless communicated to us through those particular religions.[18] What is questionable is whether Gandhi hypostasizes Religion or gives it a referential connotation in the same way as Tillich does by his use of the term Ultimate Concern.

A second consequence of Gandhi's insistence on the imperfect nature of particular religions is his antipathy to certain forms of missionary activity and the methods of conversion employed.[19] What comes to the fore through Gandhi's strictures on the attitudes and methods of certain Christian missionaries is that it is possible for religious zeal and enthusiasm to lead to activities inconsistent with the religious and ethical ideals or values one might be seeking to promote. For example, Christians may regard it as an expression of Christian love to convert others to Christ, and they may consider it their moral duty to urge men to follow Christ. But the question may be asked whether there would be any justification for the use of force in order to lead men to the love of God in Christ. Would this not indicate a greater love of dogma than a love of man? If the desired end of conversion involves the use of inquisitorial means is not the concept of love distorted? Do not means come under the same moral scrutiny as ends?[20] What Gandhi objects to is the presupposition of superiority that accompanies much missionary activity and the implicit if not explicit assumption that the end justifies the means.

It would be wrong to conclude from this that Gandhi is opposed to conversion from one religion to another.[21] On the contrary, he defends the right of those who wished to change their religious allegiance to follow their inclinations in this matter. It is, in his view, a personal matter between an individual and his God. The right of conversion is not questioned. What is questioned is the kind of methods that might be employed to bring about conversions. Gandhi's reference to people being allowed to follow their own desires, provided they were old enough to know what they were doing and were not subjected to force or material inducements, is an indication of the dubious conversion methods employed by some missionaries. He approved of the humanitarian work of Christian missionaries in the field of medicine and in the alleviation of the condition of the poor. He approved also of their work in the field of education. But he strongly disapproved of the proselytizing that went on under the cloak of humanitarianism. A patient, he maintains, should not be expected to change his basic beliefs because the doctor who cured him happened to be an adherent of the Christian religion. Healing should be its own reward and not the means of converting patients. When a missionary report estimated how much it cost *per capita* to convert people to Christianity, and presented a budget for the next harvest of souls, then conversion had become a business venture. While this might well be regarded as an extreme example of questionable missionary methods, there may be an element of justification in Gandhi's injunction to those who would convert India by such dubious means, namely, 'Physician, heal thyself'.[22]

Gandhi's insistence that real conversion is a matter of the heart, and something between an individual and his God, makes him view with suspicion the authenticity of many so-called conversions. It would be a misnomer, he claims, to describe something as conversion which was effected by fear or prompted by material gain. He tended to regard the conversion of his son Harilal to Islam as something that was prompted by monetary considerations, and in the case of such converts, he maintains that they should be re-admitted to Hinduism without hesitation if they so desired and truly repented of their erroneous actions.

The unacceptability of certain conversion methods is accentuated for Gandhi by his belief that all religions have elements of truth and error and that no particular religion can lay claim to a monopoly of the truth. His respect for other faiths is as strong as it is for his own faith. All faiths, he claims, are necessary for the people to whom they are revealed. The Scriptures of all faiths are equally inspired, though none can be regarded as literally inspired. His response to a Christian who might approach him with the request to convert to Hinduism would be to urge him to try to be a good Christian since the Gītā could offer him no more than the Bible.[23]

Gandhi's antipathy to preaching, which was characteristic of the Christian missionary activity he was acquainted with, may have derived from his attitude to mission work in general, but it is more likely that he considered a man's life to be a more effective testimony to the truth of his religion that his words. He expresses his view almost poetically: 'A rose does not need to preach. It simply spreads its fragrance. The fragrance is its own sermon... The fragrance of religious and spiritual life is much finer and subtler than that of the rose'.[24] It is possible that the silent witness of a man's life was more in accordance with the tradition of meditation and contemplation that Gandhi was accustomed to than the more vocal and prophetic approach of the Christian tradition. But his objection to preaching goes deeper than that. He speaks of predication as a limitation of truth. For him language circumscribes and limits truth which is best represented by the way a man lives. What we have here is an affirmation of the effectiveness of silence in the communication of absolute Truth, a fact fully understood by the Buddha and his followers. Should a man's life succeed in influencing and converting others then that might be regarded as a true and valid form of evangelism.[25]

There is a clear suggestion in Gandhi's writings that he considered Christians to be lacking in receptiveness. By this he means that they were not prepared to open their minds and hearts to receive

whatever good India might be able to offer them. He urged them to
recognize that by not understanding the thought of India they were
depriving themselves of the opportunity of serving India.[26] This
mild rebuke of the attitude of some missionaries to Indian thought
and tradition corresponds to his criticism of orthodox Christianity,
which he believed had distorted the message of Jesus. It had taken
hold of Jesus and turned his spirit into a system. While it was true
that all religions were imperfect and that Hinduism was no different
from Christianity in this respect, it did not follow that the Christian
claim 'Jesus is the only son of God' could be universally accepted.
Gandhi explicitly rejects this claim: 'I, therefore, do not take as
literally true that text that Jesus is the only begotten son of God.
God cannot be the exclusive Father and I cannot ascribe exclusive
divinity to Jesus. He is as divine as Krishna or Rama or Moham-
med or Zoroaster.'[27] In Gandhi's view, the statement 'son of God'
could only be used in a figurative sense and not in a literal sense
so that anyone 'who stands in the position of Jesus is a begotten son
of God'.[28] Similarly, he rejects the claim made by some that
Christianity is the only true religion. While it was doubtless a noble
religion it still had a greater contribution to make to humanity.
Gandhi's implicit suggestion here is that it had yet to support
non-violence for, as he says, bishops still felt able to support
slaughter in the name of Christianity.[29]

   Gandhi's attitude to mission and conversion finds an echo in
Tillich's rejection of *missionwissenschaft*, an approach to religions
which sees the purpose of religious dialogue as a means of conversion from one religion to another in accordance with certain theological presuppositions. It is also reflected in Tillich's rejection of the
superficial approach to religion which sees value in every religious
tradition apart from one's own, and in his rejection of the kind of
approach that aims at the complete synthesis of all particular religions into one all-embracing whole. Like Gandhi, Tillich does not
attempt to underestimate or detract from the significance and importance of particular religions. He recognizes that every religion
has within its depth a clue to the meaning of ultimate reality.[30]
The point that might be made in this connection is that without the

particular there could be no way of understanding what might be meant by the ultimate. That is, the depth of particular religions not only contains a *clue* to the meaning of ultimate reality, as Tillich maintains, but is the only means open to man to understand what is meant by ultimate reality, for the concept itself acquires its meaning from its use in a particular mode of discourse. It would not be possible to conceive of Ultimate Concern apart from particular modes of religious discourse. Particular religions, while not embodying the fullness of Truth are necessary to convey what it means to speak of absolute Truth or Ultimate Concern.

Similar views concerning conversion are expressed by Simone Weil who maintains that much missionary activity is both mistaken and dangerous. Her position is that the person who calls on Osiris or Krishna or Buddha with a pure heart receives the Holy Spirit within his own tradition and not by abandoning it for another.[31] This is analogous to the claim Gandhi makes in an address he gave to Christian missionaries, namely, that 'many men who have never heard the name of Jesus Christ or have even rejected the official interpretation of Christianity *would* probably, if Jesus came into our midst today... be owned by him more than many of us...'[32]

A third consequence of Gandhi's insistence on the imperfect nature of particular forms of religions is his plea for the spirit of toleration between religions on the grounds that it increases spiritual insight and gives a better understanding of one's own faith. Not that he approves of the term tolerance itself. He recognizes that it might be regarded in a pejorative sense as indicating a readiness to compromise and to accept something inferior, but he uses the term, nevertheless, for the want of a better word and tries to give it a different connotation.[33] He endeavours to endow the tolerance he proposes with an element of respect. He accepts as a basic premise the truth of all world religions, and he acknowledges the benefit that could be derived from a sympathetic study of the Scriptures of different faiths. But since all faiths are imperfect, the question of the comparative merit of different religions does not arise. What tolerance does is to impart spiritual insight to a man and it breaks down barriers that might exist between one faith and another. It also enables a man to acquire a better understanding of his own faith.

'My respectful study of other religions has not abated my reverence for or my faith in the Hindu scriptures. They have indeed left their deep mark upon my understanding of the Hindu scriptures. They have broadened my view of life'.[34] Tolerance does not blind a man to the imperfections or faults of a religion, nor does it blur the distinction between religion and irreligion, but it does deliver a man from fanaticism with regard to his own faith.

'The golden rule of conduct, therefore, is mutual toleration seeing that we will never all think alike and that we shall always see Truth in fragment (sic) and from different angles of vision'.[35] The goal of tolerance and mutual respect is not one, all-embracing religion, but rather unity in diversity. Gandhi claims to be a Sanātani Hindu himself, but as he points out, his religion is not exclusive nor is it missionary in the ordinary sense of the term. On the contrary, 'Hinduism tells everyone to worship God according to his own faith or Dharma, and so it lives at peace with all the religions'.[36]

As we have seen, tolerance, as Gandhi understands it, does not blind a man to the faults of a religion including his own. Hinduism may be non-dogmatic and non-exclusive but that does not mean it is free from imperfections and weaknesses. In Gandhi's view, its cardinal sin is the way it tolerates untouchability. This practice is a sin against God and man and stunts the growth of forty million people. It is an ulcer; a poison that pervades the whole Hindu way of life creating unnatural distinctions.

'When untouchability is rooted out, these distinctions will vanish and no one will consider himself superior to any other. Naturally, exploitation too will cease and co-operation will be the order of the day'.[37] If untouchability were to be regarded as an integral part of the Hindu way of life, Gandhi feels that he would have to cease calling himself a Hindu, but he firmly believes that as an institution it has no sanction within Hinduism.[38]

His attitude towards untouchability is related to the social implications of his quest for Truth and we shall have occasion to comment on it again in that connection. At this stage it is sufficient to note his readiness to refer to the weakness and failings of his own religion which is a human construct and an expression of that which underlines all religions.

NOTES TO CHAPTER II

1   *All Men are Brothers*, pp. 56, 59.
2   *Selections from Gandhi*, p. 254.
3   Ibid., p. 257.
4   W. Cantwell Smith, *The Meaning and End of Religion*, (Mentor, New York, 1964), p. 46 and p. 232 notes 153, 154, where Hegel is referred to as the first philosopher to regard religion as an entity preceeding all historical manifestations.
5   Friedrich Schleiermacher, *On Religion: Speeches to its Cultured Despisers*, (Harper, New York, 1958), pp. 40, 54.
6   Ibid., pp. 236, 238.
7   W. Cantwell Smith, op. cit., p. 135.
8   Ibid., p. 55.
9   *Selections from Gandhi*, p. 256. In a discussion I had with Pyarelal in New Delhi he maintained that Gandhi started to search for one true religion but came to realize that it was wrong to do so.
10 *All Men are Brothers*, p. 59.
11 Ibid., p. 75.
12 *The Essential Gandhi*, p. 229.
13 *Selections from Gandhi*, p. 259.
14 Ibid., p. 258.
15 *Systematic Theology*, Vol. I, p. 242; Vol. III, pp. 262–4; *Christianity and the Encounter of the World Religions*, (New York, 1963), p. 5.
16 Paul Tillich, *The Future of Religions*, Jerald B. Brauer, (Ed.), (New York, 1966), pp. 88–90; cf. *Systematic Theology*, Vol. I, pp. 92–4; Vol. III, pp. 264–285.
17 *All Men are Brothers*, pp. 59–60; cf. *In Search of the Supreme*, Vol. 3, pp. 108–9.
18 *All Men are Brothers*, p. 56.
19 *Selections from Gandhi*, p. 259.
20 cf. D. Z. Phillips, *Faith and Philosophical Enquiry*, (London, 1970), p. 233 f.
21 *Selections from Gandhi*, p. 256.
22 *In Search of the Supreme*, Vol. 3, pp. 61–2, 69.
23 *All Men are Brothers*, pp. 61, 63.
24 *In Search of the Supreme*, Vol. 3, p. 83.
25 Ibid.
26 *The Essential Gandhi*, Louis Fischer (Ed.), (New York, 1962), pp. 234–5.
27 *In Search of the Supreme*, Vol. 3, p. 17.
28 *All Men are Brothers*, p. 65. Note the view of John Hick in *The Myth of God Incarnate*, (S. C. M., London, 1977), p. 175ff., where he describes the phrase 'Son of God' as a phrase to be taken metaphorically and not literally and refers to the claim that God can only be known through Jesus, the Son of God, as a literal interpretation of mythological language.
29 *In Search of the Supreme*, Vol. 3, p. 18.
30 *Encounter*, pp. 33–7.

31 *Letter to a Priest*, (London, 1953), pp. 29–33.
32 *The Essential Gandhi*, p. 234; cf. E. Stanley Jones, *Mahatma Gandhi: an interpretation*, (London, 1948), pp. 12, 76, where he states that Gandhi appeared to him to be 'more Christianised that the Christians'.
33 *In Search of the Supreme*, Vol. 3, p. 29.
34 Ibid., p. 54.
35 Ibid., p. 39.
36 *Truth is God*, p. 75.
37 *In Search of the Supreme*, Vol. 3, p. 155.
38 Ibid., p. 169.

CHAPTER III

TRUTH AND AHIMSĀ

In his existential quest for Truth Gandhi stresses the importance of ahiṁsā, non-violence. As we have seen, he maintains that there is an inextricable relation between ahiṁsā and Truth. They are so closely interrelated that it is difficult to separate them.

'They are like the two sides of a coin, or rather a smooth unstamped metallic disc. Who can say, which is the obverse, and which the reverse?'.[1] Ahiṁsā could be described as the means leading to the realization of Truth as the end or goal, but since means and ends are convertible terms in Gandhi's philosophy of life, to practise ahiṁsā is to realize Truth and to realize Truth is to practise ahiṁsā. That is, as far as Gandhi is concerned, the attainment of one involves also the realization of the other.

I have suggested that what Gandhi may be trying to point out by referring to the convertibility of the terms means and ends in his teaching is that our ideals not only inform the ends we aim at but also the means we employ to reach them. If this is the case, then means and ends amount to the same thing since the same moral demands apply to both in the quest for Truth. This would seem to be borne out by Gandhi's remark: 'I would say "means are after all everything". As the means so the end. There is no wall of separation between means and end... Realization of the goal is in exact proportion to that of the means.'[2] But in order for means to be classified as means in the first place they have to be something that we can utilize. The end may be beyond us, but the means are within our grasp, and Gandhi's view is, that to the degree we use the means to that degree we realize the end.

Acceptance of this position involves rejection of the view that the end justifies the means. Gandhi makes this point clear in his examination and criticism of some of the methods employed by Christian missionaries to convert Hindus. So the argument put forward by Machiavelli that a leader 'must not mind incurring the scandal of those vices without which it would be difficult to save the state' on the grounds 'that some things which seem virtues would, if followed, lead to one's ruin and that some others which appear vices result in one's greater security and well-being',[3] is completely contrary to Gandhi's views. The separation of politics and morality implicit in Machiavelli's argument would be unacceptable to Gandhi. Whenever attempts were made to distinguish between means and ends, he could point to the crimes committed in the name of religion on the grounds that the end justified the means. Given the suffering and misery that has been incurred by holy wars, crusades against infidels, inquisitions and the like, the strength of Gandhi's position becomes clearer. 'Your reasoning', he says, 'is the same as saying that we can get a rose through planting a noxious weed... The means may be likened to a seed, the end to a tree; and there is just the same inviolable connexion between the means and the end as there is between the seed and the tree... We reap exactly as we sow.'[4] Aldous Huxley may well have been echoing Gandhi when he maintained that the means whereby we attain something are as important as the end if not more important. 'For the means employed inevitably determine the nature of the results achieved; whereas, however good the end aimed at may be, its goodness is powerless to counteract the effects of the bad means we use to reach it.'[5]

If we ask why Gandhi lays so much stress on the relation between Truth and ahimsā, we have to look again at his view of the Self. As we have indicated he makes no distinction between the Self or Ātman and Truth or God. Self-realization is Truth-realization or the realization of God. He maintains what he claims is the Advaita or non-Dualist position when he says that the Self within man is at one with the essence of reality, which is Truth or God. But if the kernel of an individual, the higher Self, is the Ātman which is at one with Truth or God, then to inflict deliberate violence on another is to injure God or undermine Truth, and to cause suffering to another is to violate one's higher Self or Ātman. The basic presupposition here is the indivisibility of Truth and the essential unity of life, a presupposition Gandhi maintains when he says: 'I believe in Advaita, I believe in the essential unity of man and, for that matter, of all that lives.'[6] But is it not necessary sometimes to inflict violence and is not killing the only course open to a man in certain circumstances? Does it necessarily follow from this that Truth is impaired? Gandhi recognizes the dangers of making a fetish of ahimsā and I shall return to these questions. Here we might look at the question why Gandhi should lay so much stress on the interrelation of Truth and ahimsā.

In his interpretation of the Gītā Gandhi refers to the battle-field of Kurukshetra as the heart of man in which the two natures of selfishness and unselfishness are engaged in combat. The great need, in his view, is to cultivate selfless or detached action to the exclusion of egocentric activity. This is made possible for us by means of sacrifice, devotion and the service of others. Through the discipline of such action, that is, through karma yoga, which involves ahimsā, we come to the realization of Truth or God, for to realize God is to see Him in all that lives, and to recognize our oneness with all creation.[7]

While Gandhi's understanding of the relation between Truth and ahimsā springs from his own cultural and religious tradition it was strengthened and corroborated by his reading of Tolstoy's work *The Kingdom of God is Within You*. He acknowledges his indebtedness to Tolstoy and maintains that at the time of reading the book he was passing through a period of doubt and scepticism. We can assume that his scepticism extended to his belief in the efficacy of non-violence because he notes that reading Tolstoy influenced him greatly and cured him of his scepticism making him a believer again in ahimsā. It is hardly correct, however, to suggest on the basis of this comment that it was partly from a sense of humility, and partly from a reluctance to accept all the credit for himself, that Gandhi acknowledged his indebtedness to Tolstoy's ideas.[8] Tolstoy clearly appealed to him as a great apostle of non-violence, and one who enabled all votaries of ahimsā to realize and understand that non-violence involved not only the negative attitude of freedom from anger and hate but also the positive attitude of love for all men. Tolstoy's influence cannot be over-estimated as Gandhi's ready acknowledgment shows: 'For inculcating this true and higher type of Ahimsa amongst us, Tolstoy's life with its ocean-like love should serve as a beacon light and a never-failing source of inspiration...'[9]

This reference to the positive and negative connotations of ahimsā requires further clarification. According to Gandhi, ahimsā in its negative form involves doing no injury to any living being either physically or mentally. This means that not only must I refrain from doing a person bodily harm, but I must also refrain from bearing him any ill-will which might cause him mental suffering. It also means that I must do no injury in any form to the sub-human species.[10] Ahimsā in its positive form means love or charity in the New Testament sense of the term and in I Corinthians 13 charity is referred to as suffering long, kind, believing all things, hoping all things, enduring all things and never failing. Ahimsā means, therefore, loving those who hate you and not simply those who love you. Gandhi speaks of loving enemies and reacting to their wrongdoings in the same way as you would react to the wrong-doings of friends and relatives.[11] Ahimsā, in its positive form, reflects a great deal of the teaching of the New Testament on love and it is not really surprising that Jesus should be referred to as one who manifested ahimsā in its perfect form.

'He who when being killed bears no anger against his murderer and even asks God to forgive him is truly non-violent. History relates this of Jesus Christ. With his dying breath on the Cross, he is reported to have said: "Father, forgive them for they know not what they do".'[12]

Gandhi refers to ahimsā as his eternal creed for every activity, and as the law of the human species. Nature, he says, may be red in tooth and claw and full of himsā but man is superior to nature. He has a mission to declare and practise ahimsā in a world where himsā abounds. Man's essential Self or Ātman, is the imperishable and eternal soul, and ahimsā is the power of the soul; it is the soul force which is capable of being practised by everyone and not simply by the cloistered few. Non-violence is not meant for the saints and Rishis or seers alone: 'it is meant for the common people as well. Non-violence is the law of our Species, as violence is the Law of the Brute.'[13]

The fact that ahiṁsā is regarded as the law of the human species does not mean that it is an easy matter to practise it. The contrary is in fact the case, as Gandhi shows. Man may be distinguished from the animal by his capacity for non-violence, but it does not mean that he has shed all vestiges of the animal in him. He is still a child of nature as well as being a child of the spirit, and the practice of non-violence requires a great deal of discipline and courage. It is an activity of the brave and strong and not of the cowardly, for 'Cowardice and *Ahimsā* do not go together any more than water and fire.'[14] It is impossible to be truly non-violent without being utterly fearless, and for that reason non-violence and coward-ice go ill together because the coward is fearful at heart. This explains Gandhi's consternation on hearing that the people of a village near Bettiah had run away while the police raided their houses looting property and assaulting women. The people explai-ned their action as an attempt on their part to adhere to the prin-ciple of non-violence, but, as Gandhi pointed out, such action could more easily be interpreted as cowardice than non-violence. His antipathy to cowardice was such that given the choice between cowardice and violence he would choose violence.

'I would rather have India resort to arms in order to defend her honour than that she should, in a cowardly manner, become or remain a helpless witness to her own dishonour.'[15] While a man should never consciously prepare for violence, the latter is always preferable to cowardice or emasculation. Ahiṁsā and cowardice are contradictory terms, the former emanating from a feeling of love and the latter from a feeling of fear.

In addition to courage the practice of ahiṁsā also requires faith together with discipline and humility. The need for faith is evident from the relation Gandhi conceives to exist between ahiṁsā and Truth, and from his belief in the essential unity of all life. Accept-ance of these presuppositions would seem to be possible only on the basis of faith, and this point is made by Gandhi when he says of ahiṁsā that 'In the last resort it does not avail to those who do not possess a living faith in the God of Love.'[16] Ahiṁsā, like Truth, requires an affirmation of faith.

It will be seen that the concept of ahiṁsā poses real problems for Gandhi. He regards it as the greatest force at man's disposal, and in the end mightier than any of the destructive forces devised by man, yet there would appear to be circumstances when violence is inevitable and unavoidable as in the case of the choice between violence and cowardice. He recognizes also that whether we like it or not we are 'caught up in the conflagration of Hiṁsā.'[17] By this he means that by our very existence, by the very fact that we live on earth, we are involved in the destruction of life. It may be true that the life we destroy is in the main of the lower orders or minute forms, but it is none the less destruction of life for all that, and since ahiṁsā involves doing no injury to any form of life, it follows that no matter how careful and compassionate and self-restrained a person may be he cannot entirely escape committing hiṁsā. Gandhi recognizes this fact.

'It is impossible to sustain one's body without the destruction of other bodies to some extent.'[18] We destroy as much life as we think necessary for our own sustenance and preservation. We destroy plant and may be animal life for food, and we destroy pests for the sake of our health and, as Gandhi admits, we do not regard this as irreligious in any way.

Individual existence then seems to require some form of hiṁsā and the same can be said of our existence as social beings or as members of society. Since no man is an island it is impossible for him not to 'participate in the Hiṁsā that the very existence of society involves.'[19] Gandhi cites the example of a man who in a fit of madness goes about with a sword in his hand killing indiscriminately. To destroy such a man may be necessary and unavoidable in order to protect other members of society. Killing then might be regarded as a moral duty in certain circumstances in spite of the instinctive horror we might feel about the destruction of living beings. It would be a mistake, in Gandhi's view, to allow ahiṁsā to become a fetish, and not to kill in certain circumstances could be regarded as a form of hiṁsā rather than ahiṁsā. For example, if his son was suffering from rabies, Gandhi would consider it his duty to take his son's life in order to relieve him of his agony. Similarly, if his daughter was threatened with violation, and there was no way open to save her, he would consider it his duty and the purest form of ahiṁsā, to take her life. He justifies his action on the grounds that as a surgeon severs limbs to save life, so he, Gandhi, severs the body from the soul in order to save the soul.[20]

The problems posed by this view could be related to the question whether non-violence must always be the right way. If so it would seem to suggest that we have an absolute rule of conduct or an agreed blue-print of morality to which there can be no exceptions. It has been suggested that it is tempting to conceive of morality as a guide to human conduct.[21] Peter Winch refers to Mill's acceptance of the axiom, the greatest happiness of the greatest number, as the main principle of morality. But as Winch points out, Mill's assumption separates the person who acts from the world in which he acts, hence, in order for a person to act morally, he has to be shown that it is worthwhile for him to act morally. This implies that there is a principle apart from morality on which morality itself can be founded.[22] It is as if one is seeking to give an answer to the question: What advantage does morality bring? If the principle on which morality is based is referred to as 'acting for the sake of duty' (Kant), then that would be a way of explaining the reason a man might have for acting morally. Winch's contention is that to conceive of the relation of an act to the person who acts in terms of the Kantian maxim 'acting for the sake of duty' is mistaken since 'there is *no* general kind of behaviour of which we have to say that it is good without qualification'.[23]

The example Winch cites is from the film *Violent Saturday* in which a gang of bank robbers hide from the police on a farm belonging to a strict religious community which upheld the principle of non-violence. 'At the climax of the film one of the gangsters is about to shoot a young girl member of the community in the presence of the community's elder. With horror and doubt on his face, the elder seizes a pitchfork and hurls it into the gangster's back'[24] It could be argued from the Kantian standpoint that the elder had failed in his duty by not upholding the sect's fundamental principle of non-violence. But Winch's argument is that the elder knows he has done wrong in killing the gangster. 'It is not that he had abandoned or qualified his commitment to the principle of non-violence'.[25] It is just that in that particular situation he had to act as he did, and to have acted differently would have meant that he would have been in the wrong though not for the same reason. He acted out of moral considerations yet they could not be regarded as principles in the Kantian sense because they were principles or considerations involved in what Winch calls ' "the perspective" of the action'.[26]

What emerges from this example is that there can be situations of moral dilemma which impose limits on what it is possible for someone to do. He may be forced to act in a certain way out of moral considerations which still involves him in feelings of guilt and remorse. That is, what *must* be done in certain circumstances cannot be said to be good without qualification and might involve evil and suffering. Those who would insist on an agreed blueprint of morality, or a set of moral values, to which all our aims and actions must be subject, would not accept that there are moral dilemmas.[27] Yet cannot the elder referred to in the example be said to have acted morally even though he did not adhere to the sect's fundamental principle of non-violence?

The same argument applies to the example Gandhi cites of the madman who kills indiscriminately. One may affirm the fundamental principle of non-violence and yet feel morally bound to kill the madman given the circumstances. The principle of non-violence is still absolute in the sense that it informs the spirit and the circumstances in which violence is done and can produce feelings of remorse or instinctive horror as Gandhi calls it. Yet it is not absolute in the sense that it is principle apart from morality on which morality itself is founded or a blueprint for conduct which allows for no exceptions. Gandhi might well regard that as making a fetish of the principle of ahimsā.

In the hypothetical case of his son and daughter Gandhi would consider that he was acting out of moral considerations in taking his son's life in order to save him from unnecessary suffering, and his daughter's life in order to save her from the threat of violation. He would not regard these acts as a rejection of the fundamental principle of ahimsā. In situations of moral dilemma he does what he considers *must* be done, even though it involves him in distress and suffering. On the other hand, in the case of his daughter and the justification offered for taking her life, it might be argued that, similar acts of violence could be justified on the grounds that the ultimate goal is the redemption of souls. Inquisitorial methods, for example, might be justified on those grounds. But the attitudes and actions of those who do not believe in the immortality of the soul might differ from those who do believe. Non-believers and doubtless some believers might regard the threat of violation of the daughter's person as preferable to the daughter's death. Different moral considerations might apply for different people in the face of similar moral dilemmas. This does not change the fact that, as far as Gandhi is concerned, ahimsā informs the spirit and the circumstances in which violence is done by him. He knows he is doing wrong but it is just that, in certain situations of moral dilemma he has to act in ways that involve violence. He has to do what it is morally possible for him to do in the circumstances. He makes the point clear when he says: 'Perfect non-violence is impossible as long as we exist physically... Perfect non-violence whilst you are inhabiting the body is only a theory like Euclid's point or straight line, but we have to endeavour every moment of our lives.'[28]

I have suggested that for different people different moral considerations might apply in similar circumstances. It follows from this that what is necessary himsā for one may well be considered unnecessary himsā by another. This applies to the different attitudes taken to war, to which Gandhi himself was implacably opposed. When it is suggested to him that it may be necessary and unavoidable to kill those who oppress mankind in the same way as it is necessary and unavoidable to kill a homicidal lunatic who threatens society, his reply is that no man is so evil as to be beyond redemp-

tion, and no man so perfect as to be justified in killing these whom
he considers to be evil.[29] If it is argued on the basis of this reply
that even a maniac is not beyond redemption and that given the
right kind of treatment he might be able to take his place again
within society, the argument only serves to show the different moral
considerations that can be brought to bear on situations of moral
dilemma.

Gandhi's attitude to war is unequivocal; he considers it to be
wholly wrong. In his view it degrades, demoralizes, and brutalizes
men trained for it. With its tendency to glorify brute force it outra-
ges moral standards and inflames the passions. It is totally opposed
to the qualities of gentleness, patience and self-restraint. His opposition and resistance to war as a means of solving problems is total
and yet his adherence to the principle of ahiṁsā does not mean
a failure to recognize that there might be situations of moral dilemma in which different moral considerations apply for different
people.[30] His repugnance, for example, does not take him to the
point of seeking to prevent those who wished to take part in war
from doing so. He prefers simply to place the issues before them,
and allow them to make their own moral decisions and to choose
what they might want to do. In many ways this is an understandable
attitude to adopt, because it means that one is not forcing one's
moral decisions on someone else. But Gandhi goes one step further
than this. When those who believe in war refuse to do their duty,
that is, when they refuse to fight for some reason or other, Gandhi
feels it to be his moral duty to enlighten them as to their responsi-
bilities as soldiers, while at the same time presenting them with
the alternative path of ahiṁsā. That is, he maintains that while
they are soldiers it is their duty to fight, but should they choose the
way of non-violence then it would be their duty to refuse to fight.
Here Gandhi is indicating his adherence to one of the fundamental
principles of the Hindu tradition, namely, that one is morally obli-
ged to fulfil the functions of the order to which one belongs. He
feels that the choice is really between hiṁsā and ahiṁsā, and not
between doing one's duty or not doing one's duty. Should the
reason for refusing to do one's duty as a soldier be loss of belief in

the efficacy of war then that could well be interpreted as a choice of ahimsā.

By relating belief to duty in this fashion, Gandhi is able to claim that he would have no compunction under Swarāj, a self-governing India, in recommending those who had no objection to taking up arms, to fight for their country. Yet at the same time, he is able to maintain that the person who participates in war should strive to free both himself and the world from war. He justifies this attitude by claiming that 'one's life is not a single straight line; it is a bundle of duties very often conflicting. And one is called upon continually to make one's choice between one duty and another.'[31] If we were to argue that, as a firm believer in the way of ahimsā, and an unequivocal opponent of war with its brutalizing tendencies and degrading effects, Gandhi's moral responsibility could hardly be regarded as extending to recommending people to fight for their country, it might seem difficult at first sight to know what his response would be other than that if a man is unable to choose the higher path of ahimsā, he should be encouraged to fulfil the obligations of the choice of the lower path of duty to his country. Why he should be so encouraged might not be immediately clear in view of the demoralizing effect of training for war. If we were to seek an explanation in the fact that Gandhi, as we have seen, does not equate ahimsā with non-killing and notes the distinction between ahimsā and himsā by indicating that himsā means killing from motives of anger or selfishness and ahimsā means refraining from so doing,[32] then it might be possible to be a believer in ahimsā and yet kill, provided the killing is not prompted by angry or selfish motives and is performed with detachment as one's duty. Gandhi could certainly quote the teaching of the Gītā in support of this view, but it would still not detract from what he says about the demoralizing, degrading, and brutalizing effects of war.

A more satisfactory explanation might be that different moral considerations apply for different people in similar situations. One person might consider it his moral duty to fight and another to desist from fighting.

Yet even when a person maintains the principle of non-violence, as Gandhi does, it is absolute only in the sense that it informs the spirit and circumstances in which acts of violence are done, and not in the sense that it constitutes a rule which permits no exceptions. This does not mean that Gandhi is not aware of the wrong that is being done when acts of violence are committed or tolerated, or that he does not share in the feelings of guilt that result from so acting. What it means is that as life 'is not a single straight line' he does what he thinks *must* be done and what it is morally possible for him to do in situations of moral dilemma.

Referring to his actions in recruiting men for ambulance work during war he states:

> There is no defence for my conduct weighed only in the scales of *ahimsā*. I draw no distinction between those who wield the weapons of destruction and those who do red-cross work. Both participate in war and advance its cause. Both are guilty of the crime of war... Life is governed by a multitude of forces. It would be smooth sailing, if one could determine the course of one's actions only by one general principle whose application at a given moment was too obvious to need even a moment's reflection. But I cannot recall a single act which could be so easily determined.[33]

This remark emphasizes again the point previously made that moral considerations, which cannot be regarded as principles in the Kantian sense, are involved in situations of moral dilemma or in what Winch calls ' "the perspective" of the action'. Gandhi recognizes that in the ordinary circumstances of life we are confronted by situations that make clear-cut decisions or a choice between black and white sometimes impossible. But this does not mean that he abandons his commitment to ahimsā. He still maintains that non-violence is the nobler way, and that the prevention of the brutalization of human nature is preferable even to the prevention of his own suffering or the suffering of his own people. He also considers ahimsā to be a more effective means of liberation than revolution, because, in his view, the self-sacrifice of one innocent man is a more potent force than the sacrifice of a million men who might die while killing others.[34]

Some of the arguments Gandhi puts forward in favour of ahiṁsā on occasions are strangely unimpressive. One such argument was in response to a question posed by Margaret Bourke-White, just prior to his assassination, as to how he would meet the atom bomb with non-violence. He replied that he would let the pilot see that he had no ill-will against him. Not, he admits, that the pilot would be able literally to see anything but 'the longing in our hearts — that he would not come to harm — would reach up to him and his eyes would be opened.'[35] The response is a naïve one; but perhaps what Gandhi wanted to convey in answer to this question was that his faith in the principle of non-violence and truth had not been shattered by the use of the atom bomb. Rather it had served to convince him that the choice now open to mankind was between the principle of non-violence and racial suicide. The bomb, he believed, could not be destroyed by counter bombs any more than violence could be countered by violence.[36]

Another dubious argument Gandhi presents in support of ahiṁsā is that the course of history can be interpreted as a movement from hiṁsā to ahiṁsā. That is, it is a progression from nomadic cannibalism towards a more civilized and stable form of social life.[37] The question that arises is whether such a view of history is justified and whether or not it simply reflects an evolutionary view of history prevalent at the time. Does it not presuppose man's progress from primitive to sophisticated ways of life, and does it not suggest on the basis of a progressive increase of ahiṁsā a movement from a less good to a better form of life? The term primitive, however, no longer has the pejorative connotation in anthropological, and sociophilosophical writings, that it once had when the evolutionary theory prevailed. To understand the primitive way of life, or the way of life of a society far removed from our own, it is necessary for us to extend our way of life into the orbit of the form of life of that society, rather than bring the form of life of that society into the orbit of our own. The onus is on us to extend our understanding of that society, rather than to insist on seeing everything in terms of our ready-made distinctions. The multitude of forces governing life within that society has to be taken into consideration before the actions of the members of that society can be assessed. It would be too simplistic an approach to such a society to say that hiṁsā dominated.[38] Further, to argue, as Gandhi does, that progress towards ahiṁsā must have taken place otherwise the human race would have become extinct by now, in the same way as lower species of animal life have become extinct, is to ignore the principle of natural selection, and the fact that more sophisticated weapons of hiṁsā are now at man's disposal making the possibility of his self-destruction and extinction more real today than at any time in the past. The argument also ignores the type of considerations that might determine the present non-use of these sophisticated weapons, such as the fear of complete destruction and total annihilation, rather than a greater degree of ahiṁsā, or love and concern for others. It is difficult to accept Gandhi's argument, based as it is on an evolutionary view of history, that mankind is continually moving in the direction of an utopia where ahiṁsā will prevail.

The unimpressiveness of some of Gandhi's arguments in favour of ahiṁsā, however, should not be allowed to detract from the strength of other arguments, or cause us to lose sight of his basic position. One of the implications of the interrelation of Truth and ahiṁsā in Gandhi's thought is that it involves the welfare of all men. We shall have occasion to discuss sarvodaya, as it is called, in greater detail at a later stage. Here it is necessary to look at it briefly as a corollary of ahiṁsā. Gandhi was sufficiently aware of the utilitarian formula of the greatest happiness of the greatest number to realize that he was completely at odds with it as an interpretation of the aim and purpose of life and as a principle of morality. The votary of ahiṁsā strives for the greatest good of all, which means that he goes beyond utilitarianism. He who seeks the welfare of all cannot be satisfied with the greatest good of the greatest number. Furthermore, the methods employed by the utilitarian would always be justified if they succeeded in procuring the desired end. The same cannot be the case with those who seek the welfare of all. Sarvodaya is inextricably bound up with ahiṁsā, since an injury inflicted on one man can have an adverse effect on all men because of the essential unity of mankind. The welfare of all cannot be promoted by dubious means because means and ends are convertible terms. The utilitarian approach, if it had been applied to the political life of India, would have led to the forcible ejection of the British on the grounds that the greatest happiness or good of the greatest number in India, namely the Indians themselves, would have resulted from it. Gandhi could not countenance such an approach because it involved rejecting ahimsā and relinquishing sarvodaya. It was his passionate conviction that sarvodaya, which might be regarded as a practical expression of Truth, could only be effected by means of ahimsā, and the votary of ahimsā would be prepared to sacrifice himself in order to realize this ideal.[39]

It has been suggested that morality cannot really be understood in terms of the means-end relationship since morality may demand that we relinquish a specific end *'including the end of one's own moral perfection.'*[40] This may point to the fundamental difference between Gandhi's ideal of sarvodaya, the welfare of all, and Mill's utilitarian axiom, the greatest happiness of the greatest number, as the main principle of morality in spite of Gandhi's use of the notion of means and ends. The utilitarian axiom distinguishes the person who acts from the world in which he acts. It can be regarded as a principle apart from morality on which morality can be based since it provides a reason why it might be worthwhile for a man to act morally. Gandhi's ideal of sarvodaya, which, as I have shown, is inextricably bound up with ahimsā, cannot be so conceived. It is not a blueprint of morality to which all our purposes and actions must be subject. The ideal of sarvodaya as a corollary of ahimsā is not an absolute principle on which morality itself is founded. It is not absolute in the sense that it is a rule which allows no exceptions. Yet it is absolute in the sense that it informs the spirit and the circumstances of our actions, which means that acts of violence would still be wrong although they might result from moral considerations and moral decisions, and in the sense that the attainment of desired ends could never justify the means used to attain them.

Gandhi claims to have practised ahimsā throughout most of his life and to have applied it successfully in all walks of life. It was undoubtedly his basic creed and was bound up with his quest for

Truth. He expresses his fervent belief in ahimsā when he says: 'My love for non-violence is superior to every other thing mundane or supramundane. It is equalled only by my love for truth which is to me synonymous with non-violence through which ... alone I can see and reach Truth.'[41]

NOTES TO CHAPTER III

1 *All Men are Brothers*, p. 81.
2 Ibid.
3 *The Encyclopedia of Philosophy*, (New York, 1967), Vols. 5 & 6, p. 120.
4 *All Men are Brothers*, p. 82.
5 *Ends and Means*, (London, 1941), p. 52.
6 *Truth is God*, p. 139.
7 *Selected Works*, Vol. VI, pp. 153, 176.
8 George Woodcock, *Gandhi*, (London, 1972), p. 25.
9 *The Essential Gandhi*, p. 207.
10 *In Search of the Supreme*, Vol. 2, pp. 38, 28; Vol. 1, p. 74.
11 *Selected Works*, Vol. VI, pp. 154–5; *All Men are Brothers*, pp. 86, 93.
12 *In Search of the Supreme*, Vol. 2, p. 36.
13 *Selected Works*, Vol. VI, p. 156.
14 Ibid.
15 *Selections from Gandhi*, p. 162.
16 Ibid., p. 154.
17 *Truth is God*, p. 38.
18 *Selections from Gandhi*, p. 155.
19 *Truth is God*, p. 38.
20 *All Men are Brothers*, p. 42.
21 Peter Winch, *Morality and Purpose*, (Routledge and Kegan Paul, London, 1969), p. 172; cf. D. Z. Phillips, *Some Limits to Moral Endeavour*, p. 6.
22 *Morality and Purpose*, p. 175.
23 Ibid., p. 181.
24 Ibid.
25 Ibid., p. 186.
26 Ibid.
27 cf. D. Z. Phillips, op. cit., pp. 13–14.
28 *All Men are Brothers*, p. 92.
29 *Selections from Gandhi*, p. 156.
30 *All Men are Brothers*, p. 91.
31 *Selections from Gandhi*, p. 175.
32 Ibid., p. 155.
33 Ibid., pp. 175–6.
34 Ibid., p. 165.
35 *The Essential Gandhi*, p. 334.
36 Ibid., p. 336.
37 *All Men are Brothers*, pp. 86–7.
38 cf. Peter Winch, 'Understanding a Primitive Society', *Religion and Understanding* (Oxford, 1967), p. 30.
39 *All Men are Brothers*, pp. 89–90.
40 Peter Winch, op. cit., p. 187.
41 *All Men are Brothers*, p. 96.

CHAPTER IV

SATYĀGRAHA

As Truth and ahiṁsā are closely intertwined like two sides of a coin so are ahiṁsā and satyāgraha interrelated. The interconnection of these three concepts in Gandhi's thought is such that it is difficult to treat them separately. To analyse one is necessarily to involve the other two. Satyāgraha is a direct corollary of Truth and non-violence. It is the way in which ahiṁsā is implemented or put in action; it is the technique of non-violence. The principle of satyāgraha existed before the term was coined, and it was because Gandhi was dissatisfied with the phrase 'passive resistance' that he felt the need for a more suitable and more accurate term to designate and describe the principle he was propounding. The term that was first suggested by one of his followers in South Africa was sadāgraha, which literally means holding firm to reality or truth firmness, i. e. firmness in a good cause or in the cause of truth. It was a term which indicated the desire to be firm or to hold firm (āgraha) to Truth (Satya) or Reality (Sat). The change effected by Gandhi by the use of satyāgraha, however, makes his principle more explicit and at the same time links it more closely with his concept of Truth (Satya), and non-violence (ahiṁsā). What might be said is that the ethical connotation of the method of action he proposed was being made clear by the choice of satyāgraha rather than sadāgraha. As Gandhi explains concerning sadāgraha: 'I liked the word, but it did not fully represent the whole idea I wished it to connote. I therefore corrected it to 'Satyagraha'. Truth *(Satya)* implies love, and firmness *(agraha)* engenders and therefore serves as a synonym for force. I thus began to call the Indian movement 'Satyagraha', that is to say, the Force which is born of Truth and Love or Non-violence...'[1]

The concept of satyāgraha gave practical expression to the religious and ethical ideals of Truth and non-violence. As the technique of ahiṁsā, it put the ideal of non-violence into practice and was informed by the spirit of Truth, that is, the religious and ethical criteria that determine the way a man thinks and acts.

Prior to this term being coined Gandhi had used the term 'passive resistance' to describe his principle of non-violent action. As the struggle progressed he came to see the inadequacies of the term and realized that it was too constricted in its meaning and gave rise to confusion and misunderstanding. Furthermore, it did not seem to him right that a specifically Indian movement should be known by an English name. Apart from the fact that a foreign name would not acquire popularity or general use in the Indian community, 'passive resistance' was primarily associated with European movements such as the movement of the suffragettes.[2]

Two misunderstandings at least were caused by the initial use of 'passive resistance' to describe the principle of non-violent action, and both arose from the way in which the phrase was associated with the actions of the suffragettes. The first misunderstanding was that non-violent action was regarded as a weapon of the weak. The suffragettes were weak physically and numerically, without franchise, and had resorted to passive resistance as the only weapon at their disposal. The second misunderstanding arose from the fact that the suffragettes were not averse to the use of force or violence to attain their ends. They burned property and used violence when the occasion demanded it. So when the Indians used the phrase 'passive resistance' in South Africa they were immediately considered to be a threat to person and property in the same way as the suffragettes were a threat.[3] By the choice of the term satyāgraha, Gandhi distinguished the non-violent actions of the Indian movement from the passive resistance of the European movements thereby removing the cause of confusion and at the same time preparing the way for a better understanding of Indian aspirations in South Africa. But his choice of the term satyāgraha did more than that: it forged a bond between his actions and his basic beliefs concerning the nature of man and the nature of reality. His religious and metaphysical beliefs concerning Truth or God, the Soul or Ātman, and the essential unity of all existence, were given existential expression through the principle of satyāgraha. Hence the reason why it is referred to as Truth force, or Soul force.[4]

Satyāgraha has been described in a variety of ways. It has been referred to as the weapon of the strong and not of the weak. It is not possible for those who are weak to apply this soul force for it makes great demands on those who would use it. It 'excludes the use of violence in any shape of form, whether in thought, speech, or deed.'[5] It resists the will of a tyrant wholeheartedly but never by resorting to hatred or violence. It involves self-sacrifice and the readiness to bear endless suffering bravely. It is open, voluntary, not embarked upon lightly or without adequate preparation. It is not to be abused; it has to be exercised by well-qualified, well-prepared people, who are devoted to truth, non-violence, and the welfare of all, and who are capable of exercising great patience and forbearance. Such qualities as these minimize the risk of violence. It is rooted and grounded in faith in the efficacy of innocent suffering.[6] Gandhi describes it as gentle, non-wounding and never associated with anger or malice: 'It is never fussy, never impatient, never vociferous. It is the direct opposite of compulsion. It was conceived as a complete substitute for violence.'[7]

Satyāgraha is further described as an unending, relentless, dialectical quest for truth; it is holding on to truth come what may. It requires no physical assistance or material aid, and is capable of being exercised by men, women and children. It it universally applicable and it 'is to violence, and therefore, to all tyranny, all injustice, what light is to darkness'.[8] Gandhi claims that it *cannot* be used in an unjust cause but what he might mean is that it *should not* be used in an unjust cause.[9] He is sufficiently aware of his own failings to know that satyāgrahis are capable of making erroneous decisions. Did he not himself confess to a Himalayan miscalculation? But he points out that if satyāgraha is used in an unjust cause then only the person who uses it suffers. Since no violence is involved, others do not suffer from the satyāgrahi's mistakes, only the satyāgrahi himself.[10]

The purpose of satyāgraha, it is maintained, is conversion and never coercion. It is a dialectical quest for truth. It aims at winning

over a man by the power of love and gentle persuasion and by
arousing in him a sense of justice rather than forcing him to submit
out of fear and embarrassment. It distinguishes between people
and systems. Systems may be evil but people are never beyond redemption. Satyāgrahis may hate the systems but not the people
who are involved with the system.' The satyāgrahi must empathize
with the people he opposes and try to see things from their point
of view. At no time must he impute unworthy motives to them.
This creates charitable understanding and opens up the way to
conversion through 'a constant appeal to the head and the heart.'[11]

Gandhi recognizes the weakness of an appeal to reason alone as a
way of arousing a person's sense of justice. It is through patient
persuasive reasoning together with voluntary suffering that the
satyāgrahi must seek to melt the heart of his opponent and open
his eyes to the truth.

'I have found that mere appeal to reason does not answer where
prejudices are agelong and based on supposed religious authority.
Reason has to be strengthened by suffering and suffering opens the
eyes of the understanding.'[12]

It would not be quite accurate to equate satyāgraha with either
civil disobedience or non-cooperation although both are related
to satyāgraha. The former phrase was coined by Thoreau to indicate
his resistance to the laws of the state, and it was the title of an
essay by him which Gandhi read after he had started to resist the
South African authorities. The idea of civil disobedience had occurred to Gandhi prior to reading Thoreau's essay, nevertheless
he used Thoreau's phrase to describe his struggle against the African authorities to English readers. This led some people to maintain
that he had derived the idea of civil disobedience from Thoreau,
a fact which Gandhi himself denied.[13] In due course he substituted
the phrase 'civil resistance' for 'civil disobedience' on the grounds
that it conveyed the notion of non-violence better, but he continued
to regard civil disobedience as a branch of satyāgraha. The same
applied to the notion of non-cooperation: 'Non-cooperation and
civil disobedience are but different branches of the same tree
called *Satyagraha*.'[14]

Non-cooperation, as Gandhi understands it, does not always have to be an act of love in the same way as satyāgraha has to be, but it is an act of love and consequently a branch of satyāgraha when it seeks to promote the good of a wrongdoer. Both non-cooperation and civil disobedience imply some form of resistance to unjust laws, and could result in imprisonment for those involved. Should this occur then imprisonment should be accepted willingly. Of course, to court imprisonment, and to submit voluntarily to the penalties imposed by the state could be construed as an implicit recognition of the right of the state to impose those penalties and, therefore, to play into the hands of an unjust regime. The force of this argument is substantially weakened, however, if injustices are removed as a result of the sufferings of the satyāgrahis during their period of imprisonment.[15] In any case, it is Gandhi's view that every citizen, since he sustains a government in power, is responsible for the actions of that government. There is a kind of corporate responsibility, and as long as a government is just it is a citizen's duty to support it, but when the actions of a government hurt the individual and harm the nation it is the duty of a citizen to withdraw his support.[16] He may consider it his duty to practise non-cooperation and civil disobedience, but he must always be on his guard against acts of violence which only serve to militate against the success of his actions.[17]

We may inquire at this point whether non-cooperation and civil disobedience do not involve an element of coercion. Are we not by the use of the methods of non-cooperation and civil disobedience, forcing a government to act contrary to its wishes? Gandhi's reply to this would be that coercion implies violence, and no coercion in that sense at least is being exercised against the government. The point has been well put by Vinit Haksar: 'Civil disobedience and non-cooperation, when conducted according to Gandhian principles, do not constitute a threat or coercion *in any evil sense*. Rather they involve a refusal to co-operate with or assist an evil policy, and an offer to co-operate on honourable and just terms...[18] Haksar's argument is that a coercive threat implies either a violation of, or a readiness to violate, moral duty on the part of the proposer of the threat. It can also, in another sense, be regarded as taking advantage of the vulnerability of the recipient of the threat. Non-cooperation and civil disobedience, as Gandhi understands them, cannot be construed as a coercive threat in this sense. The satyāgrahi does not violate moral duty, nor does he take advantage of the weakness or vulnerability of his opponent who is the recipient of his actions. The purpose of satyāgraha is to convert not to coerce. There may well be an element of compulsion involved in civil disobedience, but it differs from coercion in that it is aimed at securing mutual co-operation and understanding in accordance with a dialectical quest for truth. No violation of moral duty is involved. If it is argued that a man has a moral duty to obey the law and that to break the law of the land is a violation of one's duty to one's country, then one has only to point to instances of government policy where it would clearly be immoral to obey the law of the land. Genocide is one such example. That there are risks associated with civil disobedience no one would deny, and among them is the risk of anarchy. But, according to Haksar, what has also to be taken into consideration is the risk of violence that might result from not allowing people to express their feeling and here civil disobedience might be regarded as a safety valve.

Haksar's argument that no violation of moral duty is involved in the practice of satyāgraha as distinct from the threat of coercion, however, fails to take into consideration the difficulties involved in regarding morality as an infallible guide to conduct or an absolute rule. The problems cited in the previous chapter in relation to ahiṁsā apply equally to satyāgraha. If there are difficulties in claiming that ahiṁsā is the right way in all circumstances and that the way of violence can never lead to Truth, there are similar difficulties in assuming that no violation of moral duty is involved in the practice of satyāgraha, or that it is only through the practice of satyāgraha that we show ourselves to be informed by the spirit of Truth and non-violence. The problems lie in the presupposition that moral duty is an absolute rule in the sense of a rule for which there can be no exceptions. Winch's claim, already referred to, 'that there is *no* general kind of behaviour of which we have to say that it is good without qualification'[19], is relevant here. As we have seen, acts of violence may be considered necessary in situations of moral dilemma even though they are known to be wrong. This does not mean that the person who commits acts of violence in such situations has abandoned his commitment to the principle of non-violence. He does what he has to do in situations of moral dilemma, though he knows it to be wrong, because to act differently would have been wrong also though not in the same way. Certain moral considerations are involved in his actions, yet they are not absolute in the sense that they are an infallible guide to conduct, or constitute a rule for which there can be no exception. They are absolute in the sense that they inform the spirit in which he acts or, as Winch says, they involve the 'perspective' of the action.[20]

These considerations apply to satyāgraha also. Gandhi admits that satyāgrahis are capable of making erroneous decisions and that he himself made a Himalayan miscalculation in instituting mass satyāgraha in Ahmedabad without teaching the people involved in the movement the strict conditions and necessary limitations of satyāgraha.[21] It is Gandhi's contention, however, that when satyāgraha is wrongly used only the satyāgrahis suffer since no coercion or violence to others is involved. We might agree that coercion *'in any evil sense'* is not involved in the practice of satyāgraha, and it could be argued that what the phrase implies is that no abandonment of the principle of non-violence is involved. But it is difficult to avoid the conclusion that satyāgraha does involve some coercion or compulsion when practised in certain circumstances. When fasting, for example, was first used by Gandhi as a form of satyāgraha in a dispute between textile mill-owners and labourers in Ahmedabad the intention was to rally the flagging spirit and resolve of the workers, but it had the added effect of forcing the mill owners into negotiation. It was not Gandhi's intention when he originally decided to fast to exert moral coercion on the mill-owners, since coercion in any form was contrary to the aims of satyāgraha, yet despite the unexpected result of his fast Gandhi still felt that he had acted correctly in the circumstances.[22] The experience did not prevent him either from using fasts as a form of satyāgraha on other occasions with similar results. It could be argued that this was a violation of the satyāgrahi's moral duty not to coerce his opponent or to take advantage of his weakness and vulnerability. On the other hand, it could be claimed with some justification that moral considerations were involved in Gandhi's decision to fast and that he did what he thought he had to do in those situations. His decision did not mean that he had abandoned his commitment to persuasion and conversion; it was the principle of non-violence and not coercion which informed the spirit of his actions. Yet some form of coercion or compulsion still resulted from what he considered it right for him to do in certain circumstances.

Gandhi recognizes that satyāgraha requires self-discipline and dedication hence his insistence on high moral standards and adequate training for prospective satyāgrahis. It corresponds to what Gandhi conceives to be necessary in the quest for Truth. No monastic or holy order within the Christian tradition demands greater dedication and discipline, and the basic requirements of a satyāgrahi correspond to the vows of poverty, chastity and obedience, that are expected of certain Christian orders of monks and priests.

The vow of poverty within the Indian tradition takes the form of non-possession (aparigraha). The satyāgrahi must not desire anything that is beyond the reach of the most unfortunate of human beings. He should take no thought for the morrow, and should bear in mind that possessions imply making provision for the future. No seeker after truth should doubt that his daily bread will be provided. From the absolute standpoint, even a man's body has to be regarded as a possession, so dedicated use of the body in the service of others is the highest ideal and the most effective means of happiness. It is not possible to reconcile love and possessions. So theoretically 'a man can only exercise perfect love, and be completely dispossessed, if he is prepared to embrace death and renounce his body for the sake of human service'.[23] From a practical point of view, however, since man never attains the ideal of perfect love, he will retain possession of his body while striving continually for that perfection of love which does not shrink from making the ultimate sacrifice. What this implies is that perfect love is impossible within the realm of empirical existence in the same way as absolute Truth and absolute ahimsā are impossible. Yet the ideal of perfect love still informs the spirit in which we live directing our thoughts and actions.

It will be seen that much Christian teaching on love is reflected in what has been outlined above, and that Gandhi's teaching concerning non-possession goes beyond what is normally considered to be involved in the vow of poverty in certain Christian orders.

The vow of chastity within the Indian tradition takes the form of brahmacārya, which means literally, conduct conducive to the attainment of Brahman or Truth, or the way of life which leads to God. The kind of disciplined life envisaged by brahmacārya involves control of all the senses and is not confined to sexual control, although Gandhi did deal in detail with that aspect of brahmacārya. It may be better understood if it is set in the context of Hindu teaching concerning the different orders or āśramas of society corresponding to the different stages of life. According to the classical Hindu tradition, Hindu life consists of four main stages.

First, Brahmacārya, the student stage, which involves the study of the Vedas in accordance with the requirements of caste.

Second, Grhastha, the householder stage, which involves marriage, raising a family, and fulfilling social obligations within the caste structure.

Third, Vanaprastha, the forest-dwelling stage, which involves withdrawal from the normal requirements of social and family life, after the fulfilment of all necessary obligations, to a place of solitude for study and meditation.

Fourth, Saṁnyāsa, the ascetic stage, which involves abandoning all attachment to worldly things.

The majority of people never progress beyond the householder stage. The third stage is for the disciplined few, and the final stage is for the select few who desire the bliss and blessedness of complete union with God. The Laws of Manu, an ancient law book of the Hindu way of life, which discusses the customs, conventions and

laws, that should operate at each stage of life and govern the relation of the different orders with one another, regards the four
āśramas as the best means of attaining co-operation for the common good. It gives pride of place, however to the householder,
whose order supports the other three.

'As all living creatures subsist by receiving support from air,
even so (the members of) all orders subsist by receiving support
from the householder.'[24] It is the one order that allows full scope
for realizing the three main aims of life, kāma (love), artha (wealth),
and dharma (duty or righteousness). It is evident that the classical
Hindu tradition, in which Gandhi was nurtured, recognized the
importance of family life as providing the cohesive force required
for the well-being of society as a whole. Gandhi acknowledged this
and what he has to say about brahmacārya has to be taken as
applying in the main to those who are able to accept the discipline
involved in resolving to enter the third stage of life. According to
the Laws of Manu, a vānaprasthin must control his senses, keep
his organs in subjection, abandon his belongings, commit his wife
to his sons or allow her to accompany him, be chaste, patient,
friendly, and compassionate towards all creatures.[25]

When Gandhi, with the consent of his wife, took the brahmacārya vow, he regarded himself as having advanced to the vanaprastha stage of life. The brahmacārya vow evidently differs from
the brahmacārya stage of life since different obligations and obser-
vances are involved. The literal meaning of brahmacārya is the
same in both cases, but the discipline required of one who resolves
to become a vānaprasthin, differs from that required of the student. The reason Gandhi gives for choosing to become a vānaprasthin is that he wanted to devote himself to the service of the community.[26] This means that he did not consider that by taking the
brahmacārya vow he was necessarily withdrawing from the life
of society, which was one reason why he resented being called
an ascetic.[27] The saṁnyāsin after all, adopts a negative attitude
to empirical existence while the vānaprasthin is more positive
in his approach to the empirical. The saṁnyasin seeks release from
saṁsāra, the endless round of birth, death and rebirth; he renoun-

ces the world in favour of mystical union with God. The vāna-prasthin on the other hand, seeks to realize Truth existentially in and through the service of others. Gandhi interprets his pro-gression to the third stage of life as an extension of his social oblig-ations. As family obligations recede to some extent, so his com-mitment to Truth and ahiṁsā increases through the service of his fellow men. Commenting on his sexual abstinence Erik Erikson writes: 'It is of importance here that he gave up sexual intimacy for a wider communal intimacy and not just because sexuality seemed immoral in any Calvinistic sense. The sexual life (at least for him) seemed to becloud the sense of unerring craftmanship needed for the creation of the new instrument of peace, Satyag-raha.'[28] This assessment is borne out in part by what Gandhi himself says about the need for sexual renunciation in order to realize God.

From the description of the requirements of the vanaprastha āśrama contained in the Laws of Manu, we see that it involves abandoning possession, a fact we noted in connection with the requirements of a satyāgrahi. It also involves control of the senses, including sexual control, which Gandhi regards as another require-ment of the true satyāgrahi.

'The man, who is wedded to Truth and worships Truth alone, proves unfaithful to her, if he applies his talents to anything else. How then can he minister to the senses?... Realization of Truth through self-gratification should...appear a contradiction in terms.'[29]

Chastity is referred to as one of the greatest disciplines. It gives stamina and firmness of purpose by conserving vital energy. But physical control is of no value without mental control, for whoever lusts in thought remains permanently unsatiated.[30] The brahmacārin, however, is unaffected by temptation, in the same way as the marble statue of a man is unaffected by the presence of a beautiful woman. At no time should a true satyāgrahi or a brahmacārin seek to avoid the company of women, but whether this justifies him in openly seeking the company of women in order to prove the strength of his brahmacārya vow, as Gandhi himself occasionally did, is a highly debatable point. On the other hand, to magnify this incident in the life of Gandhi out of all proportion to its significance is also a questionable enterprise.

The question that arises is whether Gandhi's emphasis on brahmacārya, in the sense of sexual control, meant that married men were excluded from taking the vow. The fact that Gandhi remained a married man despite taking the brahmacārya vow indicates that this is not the case.

Gandhi's injunction is that a married couple should act as if they are unmarried, and treat each other as brother and sister. By this he means that they should refrain from sexual intercourse, for no satyāgrahi should desire progeny, which, in Gandhi's view, is the only legitimate reason for sexual intercourse. 'Realization of God', he claims, 'is impossible without complete renunciation of the sexual desire.'[31] So a married man who wishes to become a satyāgrahi requires the consent of his wife since her rights have to be taken into consideration in this matter.

It needs to be reiterated that the brahmacārya vow is what is required of those men who choose to become satyāgrahis and not something that is required of all men. Gandhi has no aversion to sex and refers to it as 'a fine and noble thing', but he insists that 'it is meant only for the act of creation'. In fact, when the sex act takes place only when progeny is desired then it can be referred to as married brahmacārya. For this reason, he is unable to support birth control by means of contraceptives, but he would have no hesitation in recommending self-control.[32] This seems to indicate that, despite his reference to sex as a fine and noble thing, he still regards it with a certain amount of misgiving, and as something that should be kept under strict control. He clearly has a highly unrealistic view of human nature if he assumes that sexual activity will only take place when progeny is desired. It is also difficult to see the consistency between his reference to sex as fine and noble and his claim that only complete renunciation of sex leads to the realization of God.

Among the aids for the observance of brahmachārya Gandhi mentions the importance of diet, and the avoidance of overindulgence. Fasting and abstention from intoxicating drink and drugs is also invaluable since the senses can only be kept under control when they are contained.[33]

The vow of obedience characteristic of the Christian orders can be equated within the Indian tradition with the obedience required to abide by the rules governing non-violent action. The satyāgrahi, for example, is required to harbour no anger, never retaliate, voluntarily submit to arrest, never resort to insults, behave courteously, obey orders, respect the religious beliefs of others, be prepared to suffer and be scrupulously honest. The man who wishes to realize Truth 'must be completely free from anger and lust, greed and attachment, pride and fear. He must reduce himself to zero and have perfect control over all his senses...'.[34] He is also expected to have complete trust in his opponent in spite of all indications to the contrary.

'Even if the opponent plays him false twenty times, the *Satyagrahi* is ready to trust him the twenty-first time, for an implicit trust in human nature is the very essence of his creed.'[35] What sustains him constantly is belief in God or Truth, for the strength of a satyāgrahi is firmly rooted in faith and prayer. Only thus can he overcome evil by good, anger by love, untruth by truth and himsā by ahimsā. The importance of the ideal is evident here. Although it may prove unattainable it still informs the spirit in which he lives.

The technique of satyāgraha was applied successfully by Gandhi on many occasions. It was applied against the discriminatory laws of the Transvaal Government, one of which required Indians to procure a certificate of registration from the Registrar of Asiatics or else face the threat of deportation. Another law declared Hindu, Muslim and Parsee marriages to be illegal. On this occasion, satyāgraha involved the imprisonment of thousands of Indians, much to the embarrassment of the Union Government of South Africa.

Satyāgraha was applied against the British indigo planters at Champaran in Bihar, where peasant cultivators, or ryots, were being unfairly treated. It was also brought to bear on the disputes between the textile mill-owners and labourers in Ahmedabad, and involved a strike by the workers. It was on this occasion, as we have seen, that Gandhi for the first time resorted to fasting as a form of satyāgraha. The coercive aspect of fasting has already been referred to. Gandhi himself claimed that his purpose in fasting was to take upon himself the burden of the workers; he was identifying himself with them and sharing their despair, frustration and suffering. His understanding of fasting is that it should be regarded as a form of self-imposed suffering. If it is directed against an opponent it ceases to be self-suffering and becomes instead a form of coercion, which is an aspect of violence, and as such unacceptable. No fast should be undertaken against an opponent; it should be undertaken rather for the good of those near and dear to the person who fasts.

'Fasting can be resorted to only against a lover, not to extort rights but to reform him, as when a son fasts for a father who drinks... I fasted to reform those who loved me.'[36] Whenever a fast is undertaken for selfish ends it must be resisted. The dividing line between altruistic and selfish ends is often thin, but any person who considers the aim of a fast to be selfish should not yield to its pressure, even though the person engaged in the fast might die as a result.[37] The kind of occasion when this injunction might apply would be when a prisoner deliberately fasts to bring about a change in his status, or else to cause the maximum amount of embarrassment to the authorities. It is interesting to note that it is the present policy of some authorities to allow such a prisoner to die rather than to submit him to the indignity of forcible feeding. In this respect, they may be regarded as following Gandhi's suggestions and advice.

Satyāgraha was resorted to in the case of the peasant cultivators of Kheda, who sought suspension of the payment of an annual revenue assessment because of the failure of crops and an impending famine. It resulted in a Government compromise which, though not entirely satisfactory, enabled the peasant to realize the benefit of joint action in a just cause and forced Government employees to understand the conditions of the peasants.

The technique of satyāgraha was implemented also on behalf of the untouchables who were forbidden to use the roads in the vicinity of the Vykom temple in Travancore, South India. The immediate aim was to open the roads to and from the temple to untouchables, but it proved to be a symbol of the movement to eliminate discrimination against untouchables in all spheres of life and a pointer to the need to abolish the caste system. In this respect it showed concern for the welfare of all men, and consequently it can be said that satyāgraha whenever it is implemented involves sarvodaya.

NOTES TO CHAPTER IV

1 *Selected Works*, Vol. III, pp. 150-1.
2 Ibid., pp. 150, 153.
3 Ibid., pp. 153-5.
4 *Selected Works*, Vol. VI, pp. 180-1.
5 Ibid., p. 185.
6 *Selected Works*, Vol. IV, p. 172; *The Essential Gandhi* p. 88.
7 *Selected Works*, Vol. VI, p. 187.
8 Ibid., p. 183.
9 Ibid., p. 185.
10 *The Essential Gandhi*, p. 88; *Selected Works*, Vol. IV, p. 172.
11 *Selections from Gandhi*, p. 222.
12 Ibid.
13 Ibid., p. 40.
14 *Selected Works*, Vol. VI, p. 209.
15 Cf. Vinit Haksar, 'Rawl and Gandhi on Civil Disobedience', *Inquiry*, Vol. 19, No 2, (1976), p. 155.
16 *Selections from Gandhi*, p. 225.
17 *Selected Works*, Vol. VI, pp. 211-4.
18 Op. cit., p. 180 Haksar develops his argument in 'Coercive Proposals', *Political Theory*, Vol. IV, No 1., (Feb., 1976), pp. 65-79.
19 Op. cit., p. 181.
20 Op. cit., p. 186.
21 *Gandhi: An Autobiography*, (London, 1966), pp. 391-2.
22 Ibid., p. 360.
23 *Selections from Gandhi*, p. 17.
24 Sarvepalli Radhakrishnan and Charles A. Moore, *A Source Book in Indian Philosophy*, (New Jersey, 1973), p. 179.
25 Ibid., pp. 181-2.
26 *An Autobiography*, pp. 171-4.
27 *All Men are Brothers* p. 116.
28 Erik H. Erikson, *Gandhi's Truth*, (London, 1970), p. 192.
29 *Selected Works*, Vol. IV, pp. 219-20.
30 *Selected Works* Vol. VI, p. 198; *All Men are Brothers* p. 113.
31 *Selections from Gandhi*, p. 248.
32 *In Search of the Supreme*, Vol. II, p. 83.
33 *All Men are Brothers* p. 14.
34 Ibid., p. 110.
35 *Selected Works*, Vol. VI, p. 200.
36 *The Essential Gandhi*, pp. 209-10.
37 *Selected Works*, Vol. VI, p. 217.

CHAPTER V

SARVODAYA

My analysis hitherto has shown the interrelation of three concepts in Gandhi's thought, namely, Truth, ahiṁsā and satyāgraha. I have shown that his quest for Truth is the quest for Reality or God, and the attempt to live in accordance with the religious and ethical ideals of the Hindu way of life. But no distinction can be drawn in Advaitin thought between Reality and the highest Self or Ātman, so the quest for Truth involves knowing the Self which also involves ahiṁsā for to injure or inflict deliberate violence on another is to violate the Ātman which all men share. The basic presuppositions that present themselves here are the indivisibility of Truth, the identity of the Self (Ātman) and Truth or God, and the essential unity of all existence. The implications of these presuppositions are far-reaching and affect every conceivable aspect of man's life. They clearly have social, economic and political ramifications and affect man's relationship with his fellow man: all men are brothers because they partake of the same reality and share the same Ātman.

'I believe', says Gandhi, 'in the absolute oneness of God and therefore of humanity. What though we have many bodies? We have but one soul. The rays of the sun are many through refraction. But they have the same source. I cannot, therefore, detach myself from the wickedest soul nor may I be denied identity with the most virtuous.'[1]

Man's relationship with the animal kingdom and with the natural world as a whole is also affected by this belief in the essential unity of all that exists. No violence to animals and no insensitive, deliberate exploitation of nature can be permitted or tolerated.

'To see the universal and all-pervading Spirit of Truth face to face one must be able to love the meanest of creation as oneself.'[2]

It is this belief in the essential unity of life that underlies Gandhi's

feeling of affinity with the animal kingdom and his support for
cow-worship. For him the cow epitomises the sub-human world;
it is, by its very existence, a plea for justice on behalf of the animal
world. It is 'a poem of pity'.[3] A sign of spiritual progress would
be the cessation of killing animals for food and the acceptance of
a vegetarian diet, and Gandhi quotes Goldsmith in support of
his views:

> No flocks that range the valley free
> To slaughter I condemn.
> Taught by the Power that pities me
> I learn to pity them.[4]

To be completely consistent perhaps Gandhi would not only
have to be opposed to the killing of animals for food, but also to
the killing of disease-carrying rats, mosquitoes, and venomous
snakes, and those forms of plant life that are essential to a vegetarian diet. He recognizes this, and indicates the contradiction
that must exist between a man's ideals and his practice, or between
his beliefs and his actions. He attempts to resolve the problem
by affirming his belief in the ideal on the grounds that man's
life is an aspiration or a striving for, perfection, yet at the same
time recognizing that in an imperfect world one has to make
concessions to, or to cater for, human weakness. This does not
mean that the ideal has been compromised in any way, or that
Gandhi's fundamental principle of non-violence has been qualified
in order to take account of man's weaknesses and imperfections.
It is possible for a man's commitment to his fundamental principles
to remain firm even though he may act in certain circumstances in
a way contrary to those principles. A rejection of an ideal or
principle is involved only if, when considering the relation of a
man to his acts, his principle or ideal is regarded as absolute in
the sense that it constitutes an infallible guide to human conduct,
or if it is conceived of as a maxim in the Kantian sense and
provides the reason a man might have for thinking it worthwhile
for him to act morally. But moral considerations are involved
in situations when rats, fleas and snakes are destroyed, and robbers

and murderers are killed, in order to protect the lives of others. It might be argued that in such situations it is the only course of action open to a man and that he would be at fault if he acted differently. This would explain Gandhi's claim that one should not make a fetish of non-violence. In situations of moral dilemma a man must do what he thinks he has to do and moral decisions are involved in his action. He knows he is acting contrary to his fundamental principle or ideal, but the standard of the ideal is not lowered or compromised on that account.

What this argument suggests in Gandhi's case is that he does not abandon his commitment to the principle of non-violence or qualify it in any way when he approves the destruction of life. He endeavours to make this point clear when he says: 'Though... I endorsed the destruction of rats and fleas, my own kith and kin, I preached ... without adulteration the grand doctrine of the eternal Law of Love of all Life. Though I may fail to carry it out to the full in this life, my faith in it shall abide.'[5] He accepts then the necessity to permit the destruction of some forms of life, while at the same time holding on to a firm belief in the essential unity of all life and the principle of non-violence. He insists that in the last analysis there is a fundamental difference between believing in ahiṁsā, even though it is not possible to behave non-violently in all life's circumstances, and believing in hiṁsā. The former promotes love and lessens the amount of destruction in the world; the latter promotes hate and increases destruction.

The sympathetic or empathetic attitude to the natural world that characterizes Gandhi's teaching, and the sense of identity that he has with it, contrasts strongly with the approach that one normally associates with the highly technological society of the Western world. The desacralization of nature that has taken place in the West may be attributed to the influence of Christianity. The technological control of nature characteristic of the West has been interpreted as the fulfilment of God's command to Adam to exercise dominion over all the earth and over every living thing.[6] And the process of secularization, which has as one of its

fruits the growth of technology, has similarly been referred to as
the product of Western Christian civilization and the spirit of
Christianity 'incognito'.[7] Whether these interpretations of the
influence of Christianity are correct or not, it is evident that the
growth of technology has been most rapid and most prevalent
in those countries where Christianity has been the dominant
religion.

Tillich refers to Western man's control over nature when he
discusses the relation between Christianity and Buddhism. He
maintains that the main principles of these religions are symbolized
by the terms Kingdom of God in Christianity and Nirvāṇa in
Buddhism. What characterizes the Kingdom of God, he claims,
is the notion of 'participation', while Nirvāṇa is best depicted
by the notion of identity'. That is: 'One participates, as an individual being, in the Kingdom of God. One is identical with everything that is in Nirvana'.[8] The implications of these principles
for man's relation to nature are, in Tillich's view, profound. On
the basis of the principle of participation, for example, it is possible
for man to justify controlling nature and using it for his own ends.
On the basis of the principle of identity on the other hand, no
subjection of nature can take place, since man identifies himself
with the processes of nature. Where Buddhist influence predominates, the principle of identity finds expression. And, as Tillich
points out, the same principle of identity is to be found in Hinduism,
which is what one would naturally expect, given that Buddhism
had its origin in the soil of Hinduism. The principle of identity
in Hinduism, Tillich maintains, finds expression in the prohibition
of the killing of animals, which he relates also to the belief that
in order to fulfil his karma a man may find himself reincarnated
in animal form.[9] The implication here is, that a man desists from
killing animals out of fear that he may be killing a reincarnated
soul, but while it may be possible to draw that conclusion, the
principle of identity clearly goes much deeper than that, and in
fact it could be said to contradict Tillich's suggestion since that
is no more than enlightened self-interest. Tillich would undoubtedly
agree with Gandhi, however, that what the principle of identity

really implies is the essential unity of all that exists. It is this that prompts a deep feeling of compassion for the sub-human world and for all our fellow men.

Tillich distinguishes between the Buddhist concept of compassion on the one hand, and the Christian concept of love in the sense of agape on the other. He claims that agape, as understood in the Christian context, accepts the unacceptable and attempts to change or transform both man and society thereby exemplifying the principle of participation. Compassion, as understood in the Buddhist context, shows no impetus or desire to transform man directly, or to change him indirectly by effecting a change in his social environment. Tillich concludes from this that even the most profound expression of compassion within Buddhism cannot be compared with agape because it lacks the power to accept the unacceptable and the desire to change man and his society. 'It differs in that it lacks the double characteristic of agape—the acceptance of the unacceptable, or the movement from the highest to the lowest, and, at the same time, the will to transform individual as well as social structures.'[10]

It is doubtful whether Tillich's analysis of the Buddhist concept of compassion is accurate. Transformation of individual structures, as he puts it, does take place directly through participation in the communal life of the sangha, and transformation of social structures takes place as a result of the interaction of the life of the sangha with the life of the community surrounding it. If what Tillich says of the Buddhist concept of compassion were taken to apply also to the Hindu concept of compassion, then his assessment is equally inaccurate in that context. As Gandhi shows clearly, the purpose of satyāgraha, which is the technique of ahiṁsā, which in turn in its positive connotation means the love that endures all things and never fails, is to convert and not to coerce those against which it is directed. It aims, as we have shown, at winning a man over by the power of love and gentle persuasion and by arousing in him a sense of justice rather than by forcing him to submit out of fear and embarrassment. Saty-āgraha also effects a transformation in social structures as the examples I have given of its application in South Africa and India clearly show.

Tillich speaks further about the significance of agape when he refers to man's relation to himself. He maintains that man's sense of alienation from his fellow men is an expression of his alienation from himself. The feeling of self-contempt that follows from his alienation from himself, together with a sense of meaninglessness and anxiety, indicates the depth of his estrangement from the Ground of Being. The answer to the problem of anxiety and meaninglessness which is derived from this sense of estrangement, is to be found through love. When love comes to a man in the form of grace he has the assurance that he is accepted, and is thereby enabled to experience self-integration once more, and the feeling of being reunited with others. That is, he is no longer alienated from himself and others.[11] It is the ability of love to transform in this way that, in Tillich's view, distinguishes it from the Buddhist concept of compassion.

I have already suggested that Tillich's assessment of the compassionate Buddha may well be erroneous, and that his assessment is equally inaccurate in the Hindu context. If we look at Gandhi's teaching in this connection we see that self-alienation for him would involve ignorance (avidyā) of the true nature of the Self (Ātman). What follows from this is alienation from our fellow men because of our lack of knowledge of the nature of the true Self in others. Self-alienation and alienation from others also means alienation from Truth or God, or from what Tillich calls the Ground of Being. The answer to the problem of alienation for Gandhi as for Tillich, is ahiṁsā, non-violence and love. Truth and ahiṁsā are two sides of the same coin. We find Truth through ahiṁsā, and we find ahiṁsā through Truth. Ahiṁsā, non-violence or love, removes our sense of self-alienation; it binds us closely to our fellow men so that we are no longer alienated from them: and since self-realization is God-realization, we are no longer estranged from Reality, and we are re-united with Truth.

Clearly there are dangers involved in drawing a hard-and-fast line between the two principles of participation and identity. While it may be true to say that the one predominates in Christianity and the other in such Eastern religions as Buddhism and Hinduism, it would be a mistake to assume that Christianity is devoid of the principle of identity or that Buddhism and Hinduism are devoid of the principle of participation. Tillich recognizes the former point, when he refers to the mystical approach to nature, which is to be found in the works of St Francis of Assisi, Protestant mystics and German Romantics, and states that they illustrate an attitude almost indistinguishable from the principle of identity. He admits also that Buddhism displayed a tendency to participation as it spread out from India into other countries, though he fails to recognize the examples of participation which might be said to derive from the communal life of the sangha and so insists that it is the principle of identity that predominates.

As a further illustration of an attitude almost indistinguishable from the principle of identity in Western thought, we might refer to the mystical approach to nature of the poet Wordsworth, who claims to have felt in nature:

> A presence that disturbs me with the joy
> Of elevated thoughts; a sense sublime
> Of something far more deeply interfused,
> Whose dwelling is in the light of setting suns,
> And the round ocean and the living air,
> And the blue sky, and in the mind of man:
> A motion and a spirit, that impels
> All thinking things, all objects of all thoughts
> And rolls through all things.

The principle of identity is even more vividly expressed in his poem 'Nutting'. Having discovered a shady nook of hazel trees as a boy, he entered it:

> And dragged to earth both branch and bough
>   with crash
> And merciless ravage: and the shady nook
> Of hazels, and the green and mossy bower,
> Deformed and sullied, patiently gave up

Their quiet being: and unless I now
Confound my present feelings with the past,
Ere from the mutilated bower I turned
Exulting, rich beyond the wealth of kings,
I felt a sense of pain when I beheld
The silent trees, and saw the intruding sky.[12]

Examples of the principle of participation in Hinduism abound in
the life, work and teaching of Gandhi. In fact, what might be said
is, that the principles of identity and participation are so closely
interrelated and intertwined in his thought that it is sometimes
difficult to distinguish between them. His sense of identity with his
fellow men may be interpreted as one of the reasons for his participation in social, political and economic affairs. On the other hand,
it is equally true that it is through participation in the service of
others that he comes to realize his true Self and his identity with all
that lives. Identity and participation in his teaching we might say,
are like two sides of a coin or a smooth metallic disc; it is difficult
to say which is the obverse and which the reverse. If we were to
adopt Gandhi's style of expression we might say: seek identity,
and participation says, 'find it through me'; seek participation, and
identity says, 'find it through me'. If we were to express the interrelation of identity and participation in classical Hindu terminology
we might say that while knowledge, jñāna, leads to action, karma,
it is equally true that action leads to knowledge. Gandhi, as a true
karma yogin, would insist that detached, selfless action, which
derives from a true knowledge of the Self, is action in the service of
humanity, and also that to seek the welfare of all men both springs
from, and leads to, the realization of one' s identity with all that
lives and to the realization of Truth or God.[13]

The interrelation of the principles of identity and participation
is very well illustrated in Gandhi's emphasis on sarvodaya, the
welfare of all. He recognizes his kinship and identity with all men
and with all forms of animal life. But this does not mean that he is
able to shed his fear of some forms of animal life, or that he would
be able to practise ahiṁsā if confronted by a snake for example.
He is aware that to live at all requires some measure of hiṁsā, but

that, he says, should not prevent a man from trying to practise the ideals of ahimsā. That is, one does not abandon one's ideals or principles when in certain situations one has to act contrary to them. According to Gandhi the unity of life is such that 'if one man gains spiritually, the whole world gains with him and, if one man falls, the whole world falls to that extent.'[14]

This belief in the interrelationship of life in all its forms may find corroboration from St. Paul who speaks of the whole creation groaning in pain and awaiting deliverance from the bondage of corruption into the liberty of the glory of the children of God. Do we have here an expression of the belief that the redemption of nature is integrally bound up with man's redemption? Is the concept of unity of life in the New Testament such that the salvation of man involves the liberation of nature? Or are we simply being made aware of the interrelatedness of life and the fact that when one form of life suffers other forms of life suffer in some degree? As Gandhi says: 'whether an individual is good or bad is not merely his own concern, but really the concern of the whole community, nay, of the whole world.'[15]

By the concept of sarvodaya Gandhi really means universal uplift or the welfare of all men and not just the welfare, or greatest happiness, of the greatest number. I have already noted his rejection of utilitarianism as an interpretation of the aim and purpose of life. In addition to the objections already raised, such as the promotion of the goal of utilitarianism by questionable means, we can point to the fact that as compared with sarvodaya it shows a lack of humanity. It would be in order, for example, as Gandhi shows, to sacrifice the happiness of 49 per cent of mankind in order that the good of 51 per cent might be promoted. In the light of facts like these, if one were to judge the issue on purely practical grounds alone, sarvodaya would appear to be a more dignified and humane doctrine.[16] If it is argued that sarvodaya is an unattainable ideal, and that in the end one may have to settle for the happiness or good of 51 per cent, it could be stated in reply, that it is infinitely better to strive for sarvodaya and fail to realize it, than to start out with a limited objective and attain it at the expense of an unfortunate minority. That is, better an unattainable ideal than a limited attainable goal when it comes to the welfare of our fellow men. At least it can be said that the former shows a more commendable motivation.

A vigorous critique of utilitarianism has been offered by Bernard Williams who refers to it as 'a *distinctive* way of looking at human action and morality.'[17] Utilitarianism, he maintains, is consequentialist and eudaemonistic. By consequentialist he means that the moral value or justification of any action is to be found in its consequences, and by eudaemonistic he means that actions are justified when, as a consequence of those actions, people get what they want or what they prefer. So when he uses the term utilitarianism he takes it to mean eudaemonistic consequentialism. His basic criticism of the system is that it makes little sense on the level of integrity because it makes only superficial sense of human desire and action and, therefore, only poor sense of human happiness. Another criticism he makes is that it has an uneasy relationship with such values as justice which some people would consider to be important in human life. Winch's criticism of this way of looking at morality, as we have shown, is that it separates the person who acts from the world in which he acts, and a man has to be shown that it is worthwhile for him to act morally.

The utilitarian, according to Williams, would consider a right action to be that action which, of all available actions, produces the greatest degree of happiness. Thus a peculiar feature of utilitarianism in general is that it emphasizes the comparability of situations. Here the consequentialist differs from the non-consequentialist in that some of the latter would stress the importance of people keeping their promises and would consider it better if they did. That is, they would consider an action to be right for reasons other than consequential. What makes some people happy, for example, is that they are committed to a cause or to a person; their happiness derives from something other than the pursuit of happiness. Williams argues that the utilitarian, given his empirical approach, should recognize this fact and be prepared to investigate what it is that gives these people happiness. If as a result of his investigations he finds that committed people display a greater degree of happiness than others then it would be an important piece of empirical information for him to consider. He might also inquire how a man can come to regard that which is the main purpose of his life as dispensable just in order to fit into the utilitarian formula. Is it not an attack upon the integrity of a man to alienate him from those actions which spring from his deep convictions in order that he might fit in with utilitarian calculations? Williams maintains that utilitarianism is 'A system of social decision which is indifferent to issues of justice or equity.'[18] It may be simpler for utilitarianism to neglect or ignore the demands of justice and equity, but that is no argument for maintaining that there should not be justice and equity. If utilitarianism has no way of making equity matter, it does not follow that equity is unimportant or insignificant. The utilitarian may argue that everything is imperfect and that half a loaf is better than no bread. But, according to Williams, this argument gives utilitarian methods greater prestige and a greater role in decision-making than they actually deserve.[19]

This critique of utilitarianism would seem to support Gandhi's contention that in comparison with sarvodaya utilitarianism shows a lack of dignity and humanity. Gandhi used the term sarvodaya as the title of a Gujarati translation of Ruskin's *Unto This Last* which greatly influenced him. He summarized the teaching of that work under three headings:

> First. The good of the individual is contained in the good of all.
> Second. A lawyer's work has the same value as that of a barber in that all men have the same right to earn a living from their labour.
> Third. A life of labour where one works with one's hands is the life worth living.

The first point reflects Gandhi's teaching concerning the unity of all existence. The second and third points were taken up by him and expressed in different ways in his pronouncements on political and economic issues. These points will be dealt with at a later stage when we come to look at the social, political and economic implications of Gandhi's teaching. Here we can examine further some of the moral implications of belief in the interrelation of life in all its forms.

Gandhi's understanding of Truth and the essential unity of all that exists means that he has not only to realize his highest Self or Ātman but also recognize his oneness with all his fellow men and with all sub-human forms of life. What can be deduced from this is that religion as he understands it involves belief in an ordered moral government of the whole universe and in the fact that religious and ethical ideals should inform all our actions. Religion is not an individualistic affair; it is not something that concerns a man in isolation from his fellow men; it is not simply a matter for the individual soul seeking release, or mokṣa, from the endless cycle of birth, death and rebirth, or saṁsāra. Rather it is bound up with all life's activities whether they be social, political or economic, and it cannot be divorced from morality. As Gandhi says: 'I am endeavouring to see God through the service of humanity, for I know that God is neither in heaven nor down below, but in every one.'[20]

Here Gandhi is reinterpreting the traditional notion of mokṣa or liberation which is the pursuit of individual salvation or mokṣa by the practice of austerities (tapas) and the renunciation of all involvement in the affairs of the empirical realm. As a self-styled vānaprasthin, or forest-dweller, he eschews the full-blown renunciatory way of the saṁnyāsin, or ascetic, and in accordance with his religious and ethical ideals advocates the way of renunciation *in* action, karma yoga, rather than renunciation *of* action. In this respect he was faithful to the specific teaching of the Gītā on the need for detached or selfless action, and he may well be reflecting the stress on dharma, or duty, characteristic of the Hindu tradition and which received particular emphasis in the Buddhist tradition. For Gandhi, religion is equivalent to helping the helpless, and given the choice between 'counting beads or turning the wheel', he would choose the wheel if it meant alleviating poverty and starvation. His passion to serve the underprivileged is such that he claims to find God in the hearts of the poor. In a stark and poignant phrase, he refers to God as the belly of the starving man and claims that to give food to such a man is to give a gift to God. To talk about

God to starving men is simply a waste of time for to them God
is bread; he can only appear to them as the bread of life.

'I may as well place before the dog over there the message of
God as before those hungry millions who have no lustre in their
eyes and whose only God is their bread.'[21] Our unity with our fellow men, in Gandi's view, presents us with an inescapable moral
obligation towards them. We have no right to possess anything
while millions remain unclothed and unfed. We must adjust our
wants, and undergo voluntary privation in order that they may be
cared for.[22]

Gandhi regards it as both inhuman and immoral to maintain
that the naked, poor, and starving millions are fulfilling their
karma, or reaping the consequences of evil deeds sown in previous
existences. Such an interpretation of the law of karma which may
have satisfied orthodox Hindus is rejected by Gandhi out of hand,
for he finds it inconceivable to divorce morality from religion. To
do nothing on behalf of the socially deprived is to him basically irreligious. The interrelation of morality and religion in his thought
is such that he regards them as convertible terms in the same way as
Truth and ahimsā are convertible terms. In a sense morality for him
is an extension of ahimsā and ahimsā is a form of morality. Like-
wise religion corresponds to Truth; it is what binds us to the Truth.
Religion cannot be divorced from morality in his view for it is
belief in an ordered moral government of the universe and when
we lose our basis in morality we cease to be religious. Morality
without religion is unthinkable for religion is to morality as water
is to seeds in the soil.

'A moral life without reference to religion is like a house built on
sand. And religion divorced from morality is like "sounding brass"
good only making a noise and breaking heads.'[23] But the question
that arises is whether it can be said of any morality that it cannot
be divorced from religion. One difference between a moral sacrifice
and a religious sacrifice, for example, is that the former is what
morality may require on a specific occasion. Moral sacrifice is an
occasion; the moral man may be ready to sacrifice on specific occasions. But if the essence of the spiritual life is dying to the self then

the religious man *must* sacrifice. Sacrifical actions follow from the
religious and ethical ideals and criteria that determine the way he
thinks and acts and inform the spirit in which he lives his life. So
we may well ask: can there be morality without religion? Are there
not many moralists who would not wish to be considered religious?

Gandhi's reply to these kind of questions would probably indicate that for him morality has to be related to what he conceives
religion to be. We have seen that for him religion corresponds to his
concept of Truth; it is what binds man to Truth. So wherever Truth
finds expression, there we have religion. When it finds expression in
atheism then we have religion there also, for Truth is the atheism
of the atheist.[24] Truth cannot be confined to traditional religions,
nor can any particular religion claim to have a monopoly of Truth,
for where that kind of particularization of the Ultimate takes
place, we are face to face with what Tillich calls demonization. Can
it be, that when Gandhi refers to morality without religion as being
similar to a house built on sand he is simply expressing in a different
way his belief in the convertibility of these terms rather than
suggesting that morality has to be related to a particular religion?

This might well be the case, but it still does not answer the question whether it can be said that there is no morality without religion.
We might pursue the matter further and inquire whether there are
not different moralities in the same way as there are different religions grounded in different forms of life. Is not utilitarianism, for
example, a form of morality, and does it not differ from the kind of
morality that one might associate with a religious form of life? The
morality of utilitarianism would certainly differ from the morality
of sarvodaya, which in Gandhian thought is related to ahiṁsā and
Truth. Gandhi would reject the eudaemonistic consequentialism
of utilitarianism as limited in its objective and lacking in humanity.
On the face of it, therefore, it would not seem possible to maintain
the view that morality without religion is unthinkable, or like a
house built on sand. The same does not apply to the view that
religion can not be divorced from a form of morality. A religious
man may not always succeed in living in accordance with his ideal
but that does not mean that he has abandoned his ideal.

Religion without morality is inconceivable for Gandhi. If religion countenances cruelty and untruthfulness it is 'sounding brass' and cannot claim to have God on its side. Should it be unconcerned with the practical affairs of men and take no action to solve men's problems it does not deserve to be called religion. A true Hindu, according to Gandhi, is one 'who believes in God, immortality of the soul, transmigration, the law of Karma and Moksha, and who tries to practise Truth and Ahimsa in daily life. . .'[25] The main value of Hinduism is its belief that all life is one, and it is not possible to hold fast to this belief without accepting that man is the servant and not the lord of creation, and that all men are brothers. It is not possible to accept the belief that 'God pervades everything that is to be found in this universe down to the tiniest atom',[26] and not at the same time accept the idea of universal brotherhood and the essential unity and equality of all earthly creatures. Sarvodaya embodies and seeks to implement just this belief.

NOTES TO CHAPTER V

1   *The Essential Gandhi*, p. 229.
2   *All Men are Brothers*, p. 58.
3   *Truth is God*, p. 118.
4   *Selections from Gandhi*, pp. 252–3.
5   Ibid., p. 29; cf. *All Men are Brothers*, p. 92.
6   Paul Tillich, *Christianity and the Encounter of World Religions*, p. 69.
7   Arend Th. Van Leeuwen, *Christianity in World History*, (Edinburgh, 1964).
8   *Encounter*, p. 68.
9   Ibid., p. 69.
10 Ibid., pp. 71, 72.
11 Paul Tillich, *The Shaking of the Foundations*, (Pelican, 1962), pp. 163–4; *The Courage to Be*, (London, 1952), p. 39.
12 Wm. Wordsworth, *Poetical Works*, Thomas Hutchinson (Ed.), (Oxford, 1973).
13 Cf. S. K. Saxena, 'The Fabric of Self Suffering in Gandhi', *Religious Studies*, 12, (June, 1976), pp. 239–47.
14 *Truth is God*, p. 139.
15 Ibid.
16 *Selected Works*, Vol. VI, p. 230.
17 J. J. C. Smart and Bernard   Williams, *Utilitarianism for and against*, (Cambridge, 1973), p. 78.
18 Ibid. p. 137.
19 Ibid. p. 148.
20 *The Essential Gandhi*, p. 229.
21 *Selections from Gandhi*, p. 47.
22 *Truth is God*, p. 28.
23 *In Search of the Supreme*, Vol. I, p. 131.
24 *Truth is God*, pp. 10, 44.
25 *In Search of the Supreme*, Vol. III, p. 88.
26 Ibid., p. 108.

CHAPTER VI

TRUTH AND SOCIETY: UNTOUCHABILITY AND THE STATUS OF WOMEN

The accusations of inconsistency and formlessness in ideology that have been brought against Gandhi have not been completely borne out by what I have attempted to show hitherto.[1] Although Gandhi himself never made a fetish of consistency, I have suggested in the previous chapters that certain fundamental metaphysical and religious beliefs underlie all his teaching and that the apparent ambivalence of his position on certain issues should not be allowed to obscure this fact. Indeed it is possible, as I have indicated, to maintain that far from showing ambivalence on certain issues Gandhi held on firmly to his fundamental beliefs concerning Truth and ahiṁsā while at the same time recognizing that in certain situations of moral dilemma he had to act in ways contrary to those beliefs.

It has been said that he was an intensely practical man unconcerned with philosophical ideas or with any systematic presentation of his ideas.[2] To some extent this is true, but my contention is that both his practical activity and his unsystematic presentation of his ideas spring from certain basic presuppositions concerning the nature of Truth or God, man, and the world. It was because of these beliefs that he acted and behaved in the way he did; his life reflected his beliefs. That is, his practical activity was grounded in views concerning the meaning and purpose of life; it was motivated by fundamental metaphysical and religious beliefs which he derived from the Hindu way of life. It is not without significance that he asked to be judged on the way he lived his life.

'You must watch my life, how I live, eat, sit, talk, behave in general. The sum total of all those in me is my religion.'[3]

If on the face of it this looks like a presumptuous thing to say, feelings of antipathy might be mitigated if it is recognized that Gandhi regarded the way a man lived his life to be of greater signi-

ficance and a better witness to his beliefs that what he might ver-
bally profess to believe. He made this point clear in his comments
on Christian missionary activity. On the other hand it could be
argued that it is quite possible for a man to have a genuine belief
and to give a very inadequate account of it. His account might be
open to criticism for being inconsistent, or formless, or philo-
sophically confused, but the fact that the account he gives of his
belief is suspect does not mean that his belief is suspect. In such
cases we have to look at the account a man gives of his faith in the
way he lives his life.[4]

Gandhi's beliefs concerning the nature of Truth and its interrelatedness with ahiṁsā, and his beliefs about the nature of the
true Self and the unity of all existence, find expression through
the techniques of satyāgraha and sarvodaya. His sense of kinship
with all men and his concern for the welfare of all men is revealed
particularly in his attitude towards, and his treatment of, the untouchables. The term he uses to describe them is Harijans, the children of God. By the use of this term he is suggesting that untouchables derive from Brahman in the same way as the twice-born Brāhmins, Kṣatriyas and Vaiśyas, and the once-born Śūdras. That being
the case they are in no way different from them and they are clearly
not to be regarded as outcasts. As Harijans, they partake of the
nature of God or Truth and must, therefore, be considered at one
with caste members of Hindu society in particular, and with mankind in general.

To understand fully the implications of Gandhi's treatment of the
untouchables it is necessary to examine the traditional attitude to
caste in India. Though it is difficult to be precise about the origin
of the caste system it might be suggested that the Āryans who
'invaded' India distinguished themselves from the original inhabi-
tants of India as twice-born as distinct from once-born. The appellation twice-born means that they were entitled to study the Vedas
and to be invested with a sacred cord at puberty. Three classes of
twice-born are distinguished: the Brāhmins who upheld the cultural
order and fulfilled sacerdotal functions,; the Kṣatriyas, who maintained the political order and performed military functions; and

the Vaiśyas, who supported the economic order and performed the necessary functions in agriculture. It is maintained that: 'The superior linguistic, cultural, and social cohesion of the Āryans vis-à-vis the various non-Āryan tribes and peoples insured Āryan domination—political, social, and cultural—over the greater part of India even more than their military victories.'[5] The once-born are the non-Āryans and are classified as Śūdras. They are not permitted to hear the Vedas let alone study them, but they have their prescribed duties and functions, the performance of which ensures their promotion to a higher caste in their next reincarnation.

Outside this four-fold division of society fall the outcastes. They perform menial tasks such as scavenging, and contact with them in any form is deemed to have a polluting effect. No outcaste could ever hope to enter the caste system of Āryan society. Once an outcaste always an outcaste; he would always remain socially excluded.

It will be seen that caste was originally related to functional distinctions within Āryan society. It is possible that differences of colour as well as cultural differences may have played a part in the first instance in distinguishing the Āryans from the non-Āryans for there are references to āryavarṇa and dāsa varṇa where varṇa has the connotation of colour, but the distinctions were primarily functional. Later they ceased to be simply functional and came to be related to birth (jāti). Social divisions and the different stations in life related to functional distinctions were considered to be of divine origin and found mythical expression in the hymn to Puruṣa, (Rig Veda x 90):

'When they divided Puruṣa into how many parts did they arrange him? What was his mouth? What his two arms? What are his thighs and feet called?

The *brāhmin* was his mouth, his two arms were made the *rājanya* (warrior), his two thighs the *vaiśya* (trader and agriculturalist), from his feet the *śūdra* (servile class) was born.'[6]

The Gītā echoes this hymn when it attributes the four-fold caste system to God but at the same time the emphasis is on functional distinctions and not on distinctions of birth (jāti).

'The four-fold order was created by Me according to the divisions of quality and work.' (4 : 13)[7]

A similar mythical expression of functional distinctions is to be found in Plato where social divisions within the ideal state are related to different states of the soul. A predominance of wisdom in the soul produces philosopher kings; a predominance of courage produces soldiers; and where vigour abounds workers are produced. This three-fold division within the state corresponds to distinctions within the soul which were created by God and mythically expressed as gold, silver and bronze. '...but God as he was fashioning you, put gold in those of you who are capable of ruling, ...silver in the auxiliaries, and iron and copper in the farmers and other craftsmen.'[8]

Luther also claimed that classes were ordained by God and he distinguishes three classes namely, the teaching class, the class of defenders and the working class. Man's duty was to serve the ranks of his calling and to perform the tasks appropriate to his class.

The growth of rigidity and inflexibility in the caste system is illustrated by injunctions concerning mixed marriages which are to be found in the Laws of Manu, the ancient law book of the Hindu tradition. The degree to which the offspring of mixed marriages were despised depended on the difference in caste between husband and wife. The most despised of all issue of mixed marriages was the chandala, who resulted from the union of a Brāhmin woman and a Śūdra man; he was automatically excluded from all considerations of the dharma or law.[9]

By taking up the cause of the untouchables, therefore, Gandhi was challenging much of the traditional sanātanist or orthodox teaching concerning the caste system. He was flying in the face of centuries of Brāhmanical teaching and deeply-rooted customs. He was questioning the rigidity and inflexibility of the caste system. It needs to be pointed out, however, that Gandhi defended social divisions in the sense of varṇāśramadharma, that is, in the sense that there were certain social functions or duties which were related to one's order or status in society. So in the first instance he approved of a society with functional distinctions based on the different abilities of different members as a way of preserving the stability of social life. He maintained that varṇa had to do with man's duties or vocation in society and did not in any way imply the notion of untouchability.[10] Divisions of the kind he envisaged were to be regarded as natural in society and no notion of superiority or inferiority was involved in any way. A man was expected to develop his hereditary skills, and thereby follow the vocation of his forefathers as a matter of course, though he was not expected to stifle his innovative spirit. It is evident from this that Gandhi assumed a person might inherit the natural tendencies and particular characteristics necessary to enable him to take up the same vocation as his forefathers and also that one form of occupation should not be considered superior or inferior to another. The law of varṇa, as he called it, resulted from a realistic appraisal of the fact that men are not born equal in the sense that they do not all have the same abilities. Some are born with definite limitations which they can not be expected to overcome and what the law of varṇa does is to ensure that each man is provided with a sphere of activity which establishes for him a place in society and guarantees that his labours are rewarded. In this sense the law of varṇa was a good thing and it was Gandhi's conviction that the ideal social order would evolve only when the implications of the law were fully understood. He also maintained that a man's acceptance of his hereditary calling would necessarily limit or preclude the development of ambition and serve instead to release surplus energy for spiritual development.[11] In putting forward this view he was probably too sanguine and undoubtedly presenting an extremely idealistic picture of society. He may have been correct to maintain that, as originally conceived, varṇāśramadharma did not imply notions of superiority or inferiority based on one's status at birth, and had nothing to do with the idea of untouchability. Nevertheless it could be argued that if work determines one's place or status in society, and if the work one does is decided by one's birth, then birth becomes the most important factor in determining one's place or status in society. It is only a short step from the functional distinctions Gandhi approves of in the case of varṇāśramadharma to the divisions he disapproves of in the case of caste and which led eventually to the development of the notion of untouchability.

According to Gandhi's opponents it was his failure to recognize the underlying similarity between varṇa and caste that led to the bitter attack on his views by B. R. Ambedkar, the leader of the All India Depressed Classes Federation, who was himself an outcaste. There is little doubt, of course, that had Ambedkar accepted his hereditary status as an outcaste he would never have become such a distinguished lawyer, and Gandhi recognizes this fact when he commends Ambedkar for his intellectual distinction and eminence and shows how silly it was for orthodox brāhmins to count him untouchable simply because he was born a Mahar or an untouchable.[12] Here Gandhi explicitly condemns the rigidity of a caste system which would condemn a man of Ambedkar's intellectual abilities to menial tasks and an inferior status in society. Ambedkar's contention however, is that the idea of varṇa is simply the forerunner of the idea of caste and that both ideas are evil. 'And what is Mr. Gandhi's *Varna* system? It is simply a new name for the caste system and retains all the worse features of the caste system.'[13]

Ambedkar's arguments were typical of those opposed to Gandhi on this issue, and the latter realized that the system of social, functional divisions he approved of had degenerated into a system of caste which, in his view, was the very antithesis and a perversion of the original idea of varṇa. When unjust social distinctions came to be attributed to differences of divine origin and when the inequitable stratification of society received religious sanction, then a system of divinely ordained superior and inferior beings had emerged. It was because of this that Gandhi proclaimed the view that the caste system had to be abolished since it was contrary to basic, elementary, moral and religious principles and positively harmful to the spiritual and moral growth of the nation.[14]

'Birth and observance of forms cannot determine one's superiority and inferiority. Character is the only determining factor. God did not create men with the badge of superiority and inferiority; no scripture which labels a human being as inferior or untouchable because of his or her birth can command our allegiance, it is a denial of God and Truth, which is God.'[15]

Indications of the depth of Gandhi's feelings on the question of untouchability are evident from his many references to the subject. I have already referred briefly to his opposition to it in relation to his recognition of the imperfections and weaknesses of Hinduism, and his conviction that if untouchability were to be considered an integral part of the Hindu way of life, he would have to stop calling himself a Hindu. He goes further, however, when he maintains that he 'would far rather that Hinduism died than that untouchability lived.'[16] Untouchability could be compared to arsenic in milk and to a poison that destroys the life of Hindu society. It is grounded in ancient prejudices and is the greatest blot on Hinduism. It cannot claim the sanction of religion because it is contrary to Truth. To say that God has deliberately set one section of society apart as untouchable is nothing short of blasphemy. If Hindus maintain they have the sanction of religion to segregate the pariah then it is possible for the white man also to maintain that he has a similar sanction to segregate Hindus or Indians. So it is necessary that we 'first cast out the beam of untouchability from our own eyes before we attempt to remove the mote from that of our "masters".'[17] Gandhi feels so strongly about the iniquity of untouchability that he expresses the desire, should he not attain mokṣa, or liberation from the realm of saṁsāra, to be reborn as an untouchable in order that he might identify himself with their sufferings and sorrows. In the light of these remarks it is difficult to agree with some of the accusations levelled against him by some of his critics. It could be argued that he may have been confused in seeking to defend varṇa and oppose caste. But it could also be argued that his conception of the ideal social order, in which every man fulfils his social functions in accordance with his abilities and is content with the status in society his sphere of activity provides him with, corresponds to his conception of absolute Truth. As absolute Truth is beyond realization within empirical existence and one has to hold on to relative truth as a 'beacon' and 'guide', so it is that the ideal social order cannot be embodied in any particular form within the empirical realm and one has to hold on to those forms of society that approximate to the ideal. This does not mean that one settles for less in the sense that one dispenses with the ideal. The concept of the ideal still informs the way in which one looks at particular forms of society. This may provide an explanation for Gandhi's strong and vigorous opposition to the practice of untouchability within the Hindu way of life. He was not content with passively accepting the fact that it was a crime; he actively opposed it and sought to undermine it by means of satyāgraha since it was contrary to Truth and to his conception of the ideal social order.

While he was incarcerated in Yeravda jail he undertook a fast on behalf of the untouchables. He regarded fasting as a weapon of satyāgraha and, as we have already indicated, his main aim was to identify himself by means of self-imposed suffering with the despair and suffering of those on whose behalf it was undertaken. It was not, as Fischer suggests,[18] a protest against Hindu maltreatment of the untouchables, because that might have made it a form of coercion, which as a form of violence would have been unacceptable to Gandhi. But although the fast was undertaken for the good of the Harijans rather than as an explicit protest against unfair orthodox Hindu treatment of them, it did have the effect of producing a spirit of penance and reform throughout India and consequently a certain improvement in the treatment and the conditions of the Harijans. It did not abolish untouchability, but it was effective in the sense that it made the practice of untouchability less socially acceptable.[19]

Gandhi's opposition to caste expressed itself also in his attempt to abolish the caste labels that Hindus applied to themselves. He wished that all members of society would regard themselves as Śūdras, which would mean that there would be no restrictions on marriage or any other issues of caste which tended to weaken Hindu society by turning men's minds from more important affairs. He relates the question of untouchability to his basic beliefs concerning Truth, ahiṁsā and sarvodaya when he states: 'The observance (of the vow of untouchability) is not fulfilled' merely by making friends with 'untouchables', but by loving all life as one's own self. Removal of untouchability means love for, and service of, the whole world, and it thus merges into *ahimsa*.'[20] The immorality, injustice, iniquity, inhumanity and soul-destroying nature of the practice of untouchability is both implicit and explicit in Gandhi's thought and, despite his critics, he has every right to maintain that it was the passion of his life to be of service to the untouchables of India.

'What I want, what I am living for, and what I should delight in dying for, is the eradication of untouchability root and branch.'[21] What this indicates among other things is not only Gandhi's desire to form a society that approximates to the ideal, but also the inextricable relation that he conceives to exist between religion and morality. Hinduism had ignored this relation and had departed from its lofty ideals and its unequivocal declaration concerning the unity of existence. The whole purpose of the anti-untouchability campaign, therefore, was to restore the purity of the Hindu way of life. If it were argued that the lot of the untouchables could only be alleviated by sowing seeds of dissatisfaction among them and thereby creating the conditions necessary for revolutionary action, Gandhi's reply would be that in the long run, the cause of the Harijans could only be served by means of ahimsā and satyāgraha.[22]

What Gandhi is suggesting by his rejection of revolutionary methods for improving the lot of the untouchables is that changes in the life of Harijans could only be effectively accomplished by bringing about a change of attitude among the members of Hindu society as a whole. So making friends of untouchables was not enough, nor, it might be argued, could the abolition of caste labels be regarded as an adequate solution to the problem. As Gandhi indicates, nothing short of a restoration of the purity of the Hindu way of life would suffice. This would involve an inner change and a return to the religious and ethical ideals of Truth and ahimsā. If this is so, then the question that might be asked is why social changes of the kind Gandhi refers to should be advocated at all since they do not go to the heart of the problem. One possible answer might be that the inner change Gandhi is proposing is not meant in any pietistic sense; it is not an individualistic affair having no social implications. It involves a change of attitude to human relationships and to states of affairs. Social change is a corollary of inner change and, therefore, although social change is not a sufficient condition, it may be regarded as a necessary condition for the amelioration of the lot of the Harijans.

Gandhi's life-long fight on behalf of the untouchables is matched by his enlightened attitude towards women. In this respect he was well ahead of his time in India. The status of women in the traditional Hindu system was not an enviable one. They had been reduced to the status of second-class citizens by laws formulated and introduced by men. According to Gandhi's basic principle of the essential oneness of humanity men and women cannot be regarded as different in essence; they share the same soul, the same life, and the same basic human feelings. Yet although they complement one another, Gandhi maintains that men have tended to dominate women with the result that women have developed an unfortunate sense of inferiority and have come to believe that they are inferior to men. It is true that there are vital differences between men and women and that the basic purpose in life for women differs from that of men, but this does not mean that women are in any sense inferior. Gandhi's argument is that women require different qualities than men in order to fulfil the obligations of motherhood, for example, and in many ways it is a sad reflection on society when it encourages women to forsake their customary duties as custodians of family life to take up duties normally performed by men, such as taking up arms in defence of one's country. In Gandhi's view, the duties involved in maintaining moral standards and a good home in the midst of bad social influences require as much courage and fortitude as those involved in defending one's country against an aggressor.[23]

Man's tendency to dominate had led him to regard women as playthings and Gandhi deplores the substitution of what Otto would call an I-It relationship for an I-Thou relationship between men and women, and the custom that decrees that even the most inferior and ignorant of men, despite their worthlessness, have been able to dominate women and enjoy an undeserved measure of superiority over them.

'Of all the evils for which man has made himself responsible, none is so degrading, so shocking or so brutal as his abuse of the better half of humanity—to me, the female sex, not the weaker sex.'[24]

In support of the cause of women Gandhi's argument is that they should rebel against man and refuse to be treated as things or as objects of lust. By so doing they would acquire freedom and the ability to show clearly the powerful force they were capable of exercising in the world. Provided they remained true to their nature women could exercise great influence and wield great power. They were the nobler sex, 'the personification of self-sacrifice', 'the embodiment of ... silent suffering', and 'the incarnation of ahimsa'. They had greater moral power, courage and endurance than men and an infinite capacity for love and suffering as their endurance of the pangs of labour in child-birth showed. They also had the ability to do more for the cause of truth and ahiṁsā than men and were able to teach the art of peace to the world.

'If non-violence is the law of our being, the future is with woman... who can make a more effective appeal to the heart than woman? . . . God has vouchsafed to women the power of non-violence more than to man. It is all the more effective because it is mute. Women are the natural messengers of the gospel of non-violence if only they will realize their high state.'[25]

Gandhi's praise of women's capacity for ahiṁsā, however, does not mean that in certain circumstances they might not be justified in resorting to hiṁsā. If a woman is assaulted she has the duty to protect herself even to the point of using armed violence, but her most effective means of resistence is non-violence even to the point of death. The paradoxical nature of Gandhi's attitude is again evident here. Hiṁsā, on the one hand is a primary duty and clearly justified, yet, on the other hand, the most effective resistance springs from ahiṁsā though it might result in death. Even if we were to attempt to reconcile these two injunctions by equating ahiṁsā with non-hatred rather than non-killing, as Gandhi often does, it is still clear that he would insist on equating ahiṁsā with total non-violence.

What is indicated by Gandhi's insistence on the absolute nature of the principle of non-violence, as we have already shown, is that it is absolute in the sense that it informs the spirit and the circumstances in which violence is done. In certain situations a woman must do what she feels she has to do in order to protect herself even though it involves violence. Moral considerations are involved in her action despite the violation of the principle of non-violence. This does not mean, however, that the principle of non-violence has been discarded because it still informs the spirit in which violence is done and can involve feelings of guilt and remorse. It is simply that in situations of moral dilemma certain moral considerations are involved in the 'perspective' of the action, while at the same time one remains committed to the principle of non-violence.

On the question of marriage Gandhi notes that the ideal approach is to regard it as a sacrament. It should be a spiritual as well as a physical union. Human love is 'a stepping stone to divine or universal love.'[26] Friendship and companionship are involved and not simply the satisfaction of sexual desires. Gandhi shows a paradoxical attitude to sex, however, when he claims that in an ideal marriage there is no place for sexual satisfaction. He may mean by this, though the point is not made explicit, that sexual intercourse should only take place when progeny is desired. But does this mean that no pleasure or satisfaction should be derived from the sexual act under any circumstances? It would appear that this may be his attitude because he maintains, for example, that 'The union is not meant for pleasure, but for bringing forth progeny. And union is a crime when the desire for progeny is absent.'[27] If this is the case, then the view that sexual union is the culmination of the act of love between a man and a woman and symbolic of, or 'a stepping stone to divine universal love' would have to be discarded. We may have here also an explanation of Gandhi's attitude to artificial methods of birth-control. Acceptance of the use of contraceptives may imply that some degree of satisfaction is being derived from the sexual act. On the other hand, how can sex be conceived as a fine and noble thing, as Gandhi maintains, in the absence of some degree of satisfaction? In Gandhi's view, however, the use of contraceptives means condoning vice, undermining the virtues of self-control and restraint. and results in self-indulgence and 'the dissolution of the marriage bond'. How the latter occurs as a consequence of the use of contraceptives is not made clear, and it may make sense to ask whether birth-control is not made necessary by the fearful consequences of over-population. Gandhi's reply to this argument is that by better management of the land and better agricultural methods it should be possible for India to support twice as many people. Yet he is practical enough to recognize that excessive propogation of children should be stopped and the methods he advocates are those which derive from proper education.[28] There is need for married brahmacārya as he calls it, that is, abstinence from sexual intercourse within the married bond. Women should also learn to resist the approaches of their husbands. Marriage gives no right to the male member of the partnership to impose his will on the female or to demand her obedience. Should disagreements occur and one partner is unable to submit to the demands of the other then, if there is no other alternative. divorce should be regarded as the acceptable way out.[29]

Gandhi's view of marriage as a sacrament meant that he disapproved of arranged marriages on the basis of monetary settlements or dowries, or on the ground of caste. He also strongly disapproved of child marriages and drew on his own experiences, fully documented in his autobiography, to show the folly of such an institution. He regarded it as a cruel custom and considered it disgraceful that it should be given religious sanction.

'But *brahmanism* that can tolerate untouchability, virgin widowhood, spoliation [*sic*] of virgins, stinks in my nostrils. It is a parody of *brahmanism*. There is no knowledge of Brahman therein.'[30]

Child marriages ought to be abolished. This would mean that there would be fewer widows because the restrictions of Hindu society concerning remarriage meant that there were far too many widows. Usually in the higher castes it was the custom for women who had lost their husbands to remain widows for the rest of their lives, but the same custom did not apply to men. Gandhi considered this to be an indictment of the customs of Hindu society and he advocated, on the basis of sex equality, that widows be given the right to remarry should they so desire.

'If we would be pure, if we would save Hinduism, we must rid ourselves of this poison of enforced widowhood.'[31] The reforming zeal of Gandhi presents itself here and in this respect he echoes the teachings of earlier Hindu reformers such as Ram Mohan Roy and Keshab Chandra Sen.

Another restriction imposed on women that Gandhi vigorously opposed was that of purdah. Originally purdah applied to the Islamic practice of veiling the faces of women, but it was as a form of female segregation that it came to be accepted by the Hindus. The main purpose of purdah was to preserve the purity of women by keeping them confined. At best it was an attempt by husbands to protect their wives from marauding male predators; at worse it was a violation of basic human rights which resulted in wives being treated as slaves, or as the property of their husbands. In Gandhi's opinion it was a barbarous custom and the arguments he levels against it relate to the question why a man should consider himself to have the right to guard his wife's purity. Women had no reciprocal rights in the case of male purity, so if male purity was the prerogative of the male, why should not female purity be the prerogative of the female. In any case it was a fundamental mistake to assume that chastity was like some kind of hot-house plant that could be protected by the walls of purdah. Chastity was not something that could be imposed from without; it was something that grew from within.[32]

Reference to chastity as a virtue that a person cultivates within rather than something that can be imposed on a person from without by means of social customs raises questions similar to those considered in connection with untouchability. If chastity is a matter of one's attitude to human relationships and states of affairs the question that arises is what purpose is served by such social customs as purdah. Gandhi seems to be recognizing this point when he refers to it as a barbarous custom. If the advocates of purdah were to reply that the custom provides the necessary conditions for the cultivation of the virtue of chastity then the question that might be asked is whether enforced chastity can be regarded as chastity at all. The point might be made that the necessary and sufficient conditions for the cultivation of chastity rest with the attitude of the person concerned to states of affairs and not with social rules and customs that might be imposed on that person from without. The social custom of purdah would be unnecessary if one's attitude to human relationships were already chaste.

If this is the case with chastity does not the same argument apply to marriage customs? As we have seen Gandhi disapproves of child marriages, arranged marriages, artificial methods of contraception and enforced widowhood. It might be argued that the social changes he advocates in respect of these Hindu customs provide the necessary if not the sufficient conditions for regarding marriage as a sacrament. But if the restoration of the purity of the Hindu way of life is a sufficient condition then what the advocated changes do is to indicate what it means for Gandhi to say that marriage is a sacrament. It could be seen to involve mutual consent (hence no child marriages); self-control and self-restraint (so no artificial methods of birth-control); mutual love (hence no arranged marriages involving caste considerations and dowries); and mutual respect (involving no enforced widowhood). The social changes advocated may not be regarded as sufficient conditions for regarding marriage as a sacrament but they may be seen as the necessary conditions for the social application of the sacramental view of marriage and for the improvement of the lot of women.

Gandhi's attitude to women like his attitude to untouchability springs from his basic conviction that we are all one in that we share the same Ātman or soul. The unity of mankind derives from the unity of Truth which is God. People complement one another. One person cannot be degraded without the other suffering, for the abuse of one leads to the abuse of another. Sarvodaya, therefore, in Gandhi's view included the welfare of women and the untouchables in Hindu society and the restoration of their basic human rights. This in turn involved among other social changes a re-examination of the educational system of the country which is the subject of the next chapter.

NOTES TO CHAPTER VI

1   Erik H. Erikson, op. cit., p. 346.
2   Both Morarji Desai and J. B. Kripalani in the conversations I had with them referred to Gandhi as the most practical of men.
3   *Selections from Gandhi*, p. 254.
4   This point was clarified for me in a symposium with D. Z. Phillips.
5   Wm. Theodore de Bary (Ed.), *Sources of Indian Tradition*, (Columbia University Press, New York, 1958), Vol. I, p. 223.
6   *A Source book in Indian Philosophy*, p. 19.
7   Ibid., p. 117.
8   *The Republic*, 100, section 415.
9   Cf. *A Source Book in Indian Philosophy*, pp. 176–7.
10 *Caste Must Go*, (Navajivan Publishing House, Ahmedabad, 1964), p. 11.
11 *Selections from Gandhi*, pp. 263–5.
12 *In Search of the Supreme*, Vol. III, pp. 181–2.
13 *Gandhi Maker of Modern India?*, Martin Deming Lewis (Ed)., (D. C. Heath & Co., Boston, 1965), p. 54.
14 *Selections from Gandhi*, p. 265.
15 *The Essential Gandhi*, p. 252.
16 Ibid., p. 253.
17 Ibid., p. 136.
18 Ibid., p. 227.
19 Ibid., p. 281.
20 *Selections from Gandhi*, p. 269; cf. *Selected Works*, Vol. IV, p. 237.
21 *In Search of the Supreme*, Vol. III, p. 16; cf. *Selected Works*, Vol. V, p. 443.
22 *In Search of the Supreme*, Vol. III, pp. 177–8.
23 *All Men are Brothers*, pp. 160–1; cf. *Selections from Gandhi* pp. 271–2.
24 *All Men are Brothers*, p. 161.
25 Ibid., p. 162, 167; cf. Selected Works, Vol. VI, pp. 482–9.
26 *Selected Works*, Vol. VI, p. 490. The use of the term 'sacrament' in this context may indicate the influence of Christian ideals on Gandhi's thought.
27 Ibid., p. 496.
28 Ibid., p. 499. ,,
29 *All Men are Brothers*, pp. 163–4.
30 *Selections from Gandhi*, p. 275.
31 *Selected Works*, Vol. VI, p. 494.
32 Ibid., p. 489; cf. *Selections from Gandhi*, p. 280, and *All Men are Brothers*, p. 161.

CHAPTER VII

TRUTH AND SOCIETY: EDUCATION

Gandhi, as we have seen, was concerned with the basic human rights of women and the untouchables, the two classes in Indian society whose treatment left much to be desired. His concern was rooted in his fundamental belief concerning the essential unity of mankind, the welfare of all men and the indivisibility of Truth. He saw that one of the ways in which basic human rights could be restored was by the provision of equality of opportunity in the field of education, and this was one reason, though by no means the only reason, for his interest in the subject. His attitude to education is in some respect reminiscent of Plato. He speaks, for example, of the education of the whole man, body, mind and spirit. The mind or spirit ought not to be cultivated in isolation from the body. Plato in his theory of education insists on gymnastics for the body and music for the soul as the necessary prerequisites of a balanced education. Gandhi, too, stresses the intelligent use of the body in order that the intellect might be developed effectively and the spirit properly cultivated. He also maintains that music should be an integral part of the syllabus of schools since it involves rhythm and order and is soothing in its effects. He speaks of the pacifying and tranquil-lizing effect of music: 'I can remember occasions when music instantly tranquillized my mind when I was greatly agitated over something. Music has helped me to overcome anger'.[1] It is not enough to concentrate on the development of the mind to the exclusion of what Gandhi calls the education of the heart and body, or the spiritual and physical faculties, since they constitute an indivisible whole. It would be a mistake, therefore, in Gandhi's view, to regard literacy as the be-all and end-all, or the primary aim, of education. In his view, it is not even the best way to begin to educate a child, which brings us to his theory of basic education.

The foremost place in a child's education, according to Gandhi, should be given to the teaching of handicrafts. Here he seems to be influenced by two considerations. In the first place he believes that handicrafts involve creativity in the sense that something is being produced, and secondly, he maintains that the sale of handicraft products enables a school to be economically self-supporting once the buildings have been provided by the state.[2] He goes on to suggest that it is possible to impart the rudiments of history, geography and mathematics concurrently with the teaching of handicrafts, and that the basic skills of reading and writing should follow later. He is attracted by the idea of the oral communication of knowledge and he is totally unconvinced that it is to a child's benefit to be forced to learn the alphabet and to read books at a tender age. He refuses to believe that this is the best way to cultivate intelligence or to build up character.

'Literary training by itself adds not an inch to one's moral height and character-building is independent of literary training.'[3]

The change in methodology suggested by Gandhi may have been derived from some painful memories of his own educational process, for he claims never to have shown, or to have aspired to, distinction in academic life. But his attempt to relate education to practical activity, particularly in its primary stages, is interesting, and shows an ability to combine the acquisition of practical skills with the art of acquiring knowledge. This is the kind of approach that some modern educationalists feel is necessary for a person to live an effective and satisfying life because of certain interdependent elements which they regard as the necessary prerequisites of a minimum educational programme. One is the need to develop a positive attitude towards work, and another is the need to acquire basic skills in literacy and numeracy. It will be seen that Gandhi combines these two elements by suggesting that the acquisition of the basic skills of literacy and numeracy should go hand in hand with creative activity in the sphere of handicrafts.

It was with a certain amount of hesitancy at the outset that Gandhi propounded his views on education, but he eventually overcame his fear of ridicule. He favoured compulsory primary education for all, including women, who had hitherto been neglected, but he insisted that it should be combined with vocational training. He

was realistic enough to see that apart from the educational benefits of a vocational approach no programme of compulsory primary
education was likely to succeed without it. The economic survival
of the family unit required that there should be the full co-operation
of all members including children. He expressed his approval of
higher education although he did not agree that it should be paid
for by the state. Universities in his view, ought to be self-supporting,
and should carefully monitor their curricula. Education in art
subjects, for example, was, in Gandhi's view, a 'sheer waste and
has resulted in unemployment among the educated classes'.[4] This
may have been a reflection on the non-vocational nature of art
subjects in general, and if so it could be argued that Gandhi may
have had a limited understanding of the nature and purpose of higher education in the arts, and that he was opposed to the idea of
education for its own sake. On the other hand, he might be defended
on the grounds that he is proposing a form of university education
which is in line with basic education and consistent with the needs
of India. He suggests, for example, that colleges should be attached
to different industries which should pay for the training of the
graduates they need.[5] This would appear to link education closely
to industrial development and suggests that an economic recession
would automatically adversely affect a graduate's educational
programme. Whether Gandhi actually envisaged that this might be
the case, or whether he believed that colleges would be self-supporting after their initial financing by different industrial concerns is
not quite clear.

On the question of language Gandhi expresses himself very
strongly on the use of English as the medium of instruction in higher education in India. In his view it had caused incalculable damage to the nation both intellectually and morally. He recalls with
misgiving his own days at high school when he spent half his time
trying to master English prior to learning science and art subjects
all of which were taught through the medium of English.[6] The
importance attached to the mastery of English and its dominance
in the educational system was such that any pupil caught speaking
his mother tongue at school, which in Gandhi's case was Gujarati,

was punished. A similar educational policy was imposed on Wales during the nineteenth century. English was made the medium of instruction in schools there and pupils were not allowed to speak their mother tongue during school hours. Those caught speaking their native language were forced to wear around their necks a wooden token known as the 'Welsh note'. This usually passed from one pupil to another whenever an infringement of the English only rule occurred and the offending mother tongue was spoken. The boy or girl who happened to be wearing the token at the end of the day was suitably punished. In this kind of educational system it did not matter if the child spoke bad English, since bad English was preferable to good Welsh or Gujarati. It is difficult to fault Gandhi's argument when he claims that it would have been infinitely preferable and easier for him to grasp the rudiments of mathematics, chemistry and other subjects had he been allowed to learn them through the medium of his mother tongue, Gujarati, rather than through the medium of English. He is also correct in his assumption that the vocabulary of Gujarati would have been enriched by the acquisition of new terms had this policy been applied.[7]

His indictment of the educational system that fostered what Gandhi calls 'the tyranny of English' goes further than the accusation that it ignored and undermined the importance and significance of the mother tongue of the people involved in the educational process. He also accuses it of creating a barrier between the pupils themselves and members of their own family. Gandhi's father, for instance, although an intelligent man, spoke no English and consequently was unable to understand what his son was studying at school. The result of this was that Gandhi soon felt himself to be a stranger in his own home and in some ways alienated from his family. He also began to develop a sense of superiority and to dress differently. It would seem, therefore, that there is truth in the contention that the imposition of an alien educational system on the Indian nation was a moral injury; it alienated those who participated in it from their own kith and kin and from their cultural heritage. As Gandhi maintains:

If I had, instead, passed those precious seven years in mastering Gujarati and had learnt mathematics, sciences, and Sanskrit and other subjects through Gujarati, I could easily have shared the knowledge so gained with my neighbours. I would have enriched Gujarati, and who can say that I would not have with my habit of application and my inordinate love for the country and mother tongue, made a richer and greater contribution to the service of the masses?[8]

It was on the basis of reflection on his own educational experience that Gandhi advocates that education should be imparted through the medium of the mother tongue rather than through the medium of English. The school, he claims, ought to be a natural extension of the home so that the impressions received at school might be in accordance with impressions received at home. The Indian people ought to build on their own cultural heritage but at the same time it was important that they should erect no barrier against other cultures. India ought not to be made a prison house simply in order to secure and preserve its own cultural heritage. The treasures of other cultures should be read and appreciated and then translated into the vernacular for the benefit of the Indian people as a whole. The diverse winds of culture should be allowed to blow from all quarters, but they ought to be experienced by India in the context of its own cultural climate. There should be no neglect of the mother tongue; no Indian should be ashamed to express himself in the vernacular. Once the provincial languages were given their rightful place in the educational system of the country and made the medium of instruction in schools and colleges Indians would regain their self-respect and cease to believe that no worthwhile thoughts could be conceived in the vernacular. It may have been because of his opposition to an alien sytem of education which had been imposed on the country and his insistence that education in the arts and sciences should be in the language of the people that Gandhi was accused of being the enemy of higher education, but in actual fact he explicitly denied the accusation.[9] Yet his view that a university education in the arts was a 'sheer waste' would seem to give some credence to the accusation.

It could be argued that by his stress on the need for a proper use of the provincial languages in the educational system of the country Gandhi was not only concerned with restoring the self-respect of his fellow countrymen but also with saying something significant about the importance of, and the need for, self-identity. If we were to apply a modern philosophical approach to the question of personal identity we might say that in order for a person to know who he is he must know himself as someone who, like other people, occupies space and shows certain characteristics of appearance and behaviour and be able for the benefit of others to distinguish himself from his neighbours, that is, from other people similar to himself. The equation of the ego with consciousness distinct from the body yet inhabiting the body, like a ghost in a machine, to use Gilbert Ryle's phrase, makes it possible for someone to contend that a person is not able to know who he is. Such a contention involves the rejection of the notion of the self-identifying nature of consciousness, or to put it another way, it involves the rejection of the claim that I am able to know who I am by referring to my own consciousness.[10] The equation of the 'I' with consciousness has been variously described as an 'illusion', a 'fantasy', and 'a misleading Cartesian model'.[11] The nature of this misleading Cartesian model is that the mind consists of thoughts, feelings, and sense impressions behind which lies the 'I'. This ego is far removed from objects in the empirical world and from the egos of other people.

On the basis of the Cartesian model it is claimed that one can know the 'I' which is the subject of thoughts and experiences only by way of introspection. That is, by looking within we are able to examine our own egos directly. Introspection, however, does not give us knowledge of the 'I' of others. We are not able to examine directly the egos of others by looking within them. If follows that we can only know other selves indirectly by means of inference and analogical reasoning.

We may ask, however, what introspection means. What is involved in the process of looking within and examining our inner selves? Is internal awareness of ego possible, and if so, what would it be like to know it? Wittgenstein, for example, is puzzled by the whole notion of looking within and examining our inner selves and he asks: 'But what can it mean to speak of "turning my attention on to my own consciousness"—This is surely the queerest thing that could be!'[12] For Wittgenstein, the 'I' is on the same grammatical level as 'he', and he puts his position thus: 'If, in saying "I", I point to my own body, I model the use of the word "I" on that of the demonstrative "this person" or "he".'[13] It is clear that the grammar of 'I' here places Wittgenstein among his neighbours, and it indicates that the use of the term 'I' is intended for the benefit of others. I do not, of course, have to use the term 'I' in order to tell myself who I am any more than I have to ascribe pain, for example, to myself by saying 'I am in pain' in order for me to know that I am in pain. I may say with emphasis '*I* am in pain' but the use of 'I' here is modelled on the demonstrative 'he' or 'this person'. Knowing myself implies that I am able for the benefit of others to distinguish myself from my neighbours, that is from people similar to myself. The condition of my being able to explain who I am to others is that I can point to myself as a physical presence among other physical presences. It is true that I have experiences and intuitions in addition to a physical presence, and for the benefit of others I can ascribe them to an occupant of public space and not to something bodiless inhabiting the body.

The basis of our knowledge of another person, according to the Wittgensteinian analysis, is that he is a physical presence in space with whom we communicate in language. The presupposition of language is that statements are means of communication which bind us together. We know ourselves and others, therefore, as members of a human community which is bound together by language. The concept of an ego inhabiting the body and yet distinct from it, is an untenable one within the unity of language. The implication of this view of the self is clear: if the self has to do with community and language then the nature of that language and community, together with its literature and institutions, will directly influence or affect the identity of the self. That is, the self is rooted in the human community. It is the community bound together by language that makes it possible for the life of the individual to be meaningful and which gives him a sense of identity. An individual's thoughts, feelings, and experiences cannot be logically independent of his environment and the nature of that environment directly influences that individual's sense of identity.[14]

On the basis of this particular philosophical approach to the concept of the self we might say that the Indian knows himself as someone who is a member of a human community which shares the same cultural heritage and the same language and traditions. We may ask whether the survival of that human community with its own cultural heritage and its own language, together with its awareness of a dimension of the past, is not bound up with what Simone Weil calls the 'need for roots', and with what we have here referred to as personal identity. Is it possible for an individual to retain a true sense of self-identity if the community in which he lives, and the language that binds him to his fellow man within that community, are undermined by the imposition of an alien culture and an alien language introduced through an educational system which is profoundly divisive in its effects?

Gandhi's concept of the self involves the notion of an empirical self embodying the real self or ātman. The real self or ātman exists within the depths of man and is limited by its adjuncts, namely individual empirical characteristics. It might be said that the empirical self is a physical presence which embodies the kernel of the self or the ātman. The fact that Gandhi's concept of the individual self involves the notion of an experiencing physical presence means that he would not quarrel with the conclusions arrived at concerning the importance of an awareness of a dimension of the past, and the significance of the cultural heritage and the language of the community to which one belongs. On the basis of his presuppositions he might argue also that for him self-knowledge is knowledge of God, which is knowledge of Truth. The quest for Truth involves ahimsā, for to inflict injury on another is to violate Truth which is in turn a violation of the self or ātman. His indictment of the alien educational system that fostered what he calls 'the tyranny of English' as we have seen, is that it inflicted a moral and intellectual injury on the Indian nation. It had undermined the foundation and damaged the fabric of the nation by ignoring the languages that bound the various communities together and by totally neglecting its cultural heritage. This was a violation of Truth which means that it was also a violation of the self of the individual and an impediment to self-knowledge. It is not without some justification, therefore, that Gandhi is able to refer to 'the enormity of the damage done' and the 'incalculable intellectual and moral injury' sustained by the nation as a result of British educational policy. He was firmly convinced that it was impossible to have any real education of the people of India through the medium of a foreign language and to the complete exclusion of the indigenous culture. This cut people off from their roots. It produced children who were alienated from their parents and estranged from their cultural milieu. It tended to stunt the creative ability of many in the literary field who felt inhibited by the alien language of education and who were yet estranged from their mother tongue. The tragedy was that under the alien educational system of the country pupils were instructed in such a fashion that their own culture and traditions and their ancient heritage were presented to them as barbarous and superstitious. If children were not entirely alienated from their cultural heritage and social background by the educational process, it was, Gandhi maintains, because they were too firmly rooted in their ancient traditions and culture.[15]

The methodological changes suggested by Gandhi for the educational system of India involved not only the recognition of the importance of the provincial languages and their use as the media of instruction in the schools, but also the recognition of the need to cultivate a proper attitude to manual labour. His stress on the importance of manual labour derived in the first place from the fact that approximately 80 per cent of the population of India lived in rural areas where labour was an essential and integral part of daily life. Education would perform a disservice to society if it produced children who were contemptuous of manual labour and disinclined to soil their hands. Gandhi's emphasis on the dignity of manual labour contrasted strongly with the general attitude of the educational classes at the time. Normally, members of these classes would consider it beneath their dignity to engage in physical work of any kind, and a betrayal of their status in society to soil their hands with tasks that less able people were able to perform quite adequately. He may well have had this attitude of superiority towards manual work in mind when he claimed that an educational system which produced such an attitude was not in the best interest of society as a whole. Secondly, it would be quite impossible for a government, however well intentioned, to give the financial support required to provide free education for all children of school age. Some form of labour, therefore, whether it took the form of spinning, handweaving, or anything else, ought to be considered as payment, either in full or in part, for education received. Thirdly, the labour experience acquired at school could, according to Gandhi, be considered a form of vocational training and therefore an additional advantage to a child in later life when the time came for him to earn a living.[16]

When Gandhi combines work and learning in his assessment of the kind of educational system that would meet the needs of India he has several considerations in mind. He points out, for example, that if such a pattern was considered right and proper for the American student how much more so was it for the pupils and students in the schools and colleges of India. He was aware, as we have seen, of the tendency among many in India to regard manual labour as in some way degrading and as befitting the lower stratas of society rather than the educated élite. Education was in some way associated in the Indian mind with status and with the more refined occupations in society. It is not without a certain irony, therefore, that Gandhi refers to the British educational system as producing or making Indians what they were intended to be, namely, clerks and interpreters.[17] The divorce between education and manual labour had led to a 'criminal neglect of the villages' which instead of being the delightful hamlets they should be, were very much like dung heaps and an affront to human dignity.[18] It was, in a sense, a disservice to India to insist on making education purely literary because it failed to prepare children for the manual work that would be needed in later life in order that many of them might be able to earn their living. Furthermore, it did nothing to promote the idea of the dignity of labour. It was a strange and ultimately false kind of educational system that created intellectuals who were prepared to despise the hewers of wood and drawers of water.[19] While it was true that these people were in the main illiterate, that was no reason why they should be looked down on, and it was Gandhi's view that, by means of adult education, it was possible to make them literate, to open their minds to the greatness and vastness of India, and to enable them to understand the political issues of the day.

The form of caste distinction implicit in the attitude of superiority displayed by members of the educated élite towards manual labourers was not simply an indictment of the educational system that fostered it. It was an attitude contrary to the spirit of Truth. It undermined the realization of God and prevented the realization of the true Self. It was an attitude also that alienated a man from his fellow man, created barriers in society, and amounted to a denial of the essential unity of mankind since thoughts of superiority and a readiness to despise those engaged in menial tasks could be construed as a form of hiṁsā, in thought if not in deed, towards fellow human beings.

The primary aim and purpose of education for Gandhi is to develop the mind and build up character. This Platonic type of education involves the cultivation of such qualities as courage, strength, virtue and self-denial. In the long run illiteracy is less damaging than character deficiency. Gandhi's advice is: 'Let them [students] realize that learning without courage is like a waxen statue beautiful to look at but bound to melt at the least touch of a hot substance'.[20]

This does not mean that the acquisition of knowledge should be despised. But it ought to be recognized that it does not give a man a sharper intellect necessarily or a greater capacity for doing good, so it should be given its proper place in the social structure and not elevated to a position it does not merit. His emphasis on the importance of the development of character poses the question whether religious education ought to form part of the curriculum of schools.

His view is that basic ethics should be imparted in the schools but not religion in the sense of denominationalism. He is in favour also of pupils studying the main tenets of faiths other than their own since this not only cultivates toleration and breadth of vision but helps them to appreciate their own faith better. It would appear that what he means by the study of basic ethics and the fundamental tenets of other religions is the kind of phenomenological, historical and philosophical approach to the study of religion that would exclude the narrow, exclusivist, dogmatic approach. In this respect he shows a commendable openness to religious pluralism.[21]

Gandhi believed Indian culture to be in the making by which he probably meant that it was in the process of development. An attempt was being made by many, including himself, to weave the different cultural strands in India into a unified whole on the grounds that no dynamic culture could be exclusive in its approach. The synthesis proposed by Gandhi, however, is one where each cultural strand in the fabric of social life is given its rightful place and not the kind of synthesis where a single culture is allowed to dominate the rest. For this reason Gandhi is able to refer to unity, catholicity and toleration as the most desirable and most important characteristics of higher education.[22] If we ask what grounds Gandhi has for the assertion that Indian culture is in the making, his reply is that Indian culture, and civilization, based on a Brāhmanic system of education, had survived the vicissitudes of thousands of years, while other civilizations, such as those of Greece and Rome, had perished. It would also survive the impact of modern Western civilization that was making itself felt in India. The main characteristic of Indian civilization, in Gandhi's view, is brachmacharya or self-restraint, and the duty of all Indians was to maintain and preserve this essential feature of Indian life and not to succumb to the competitiveness and acquisitiveness of Western civilization. When Gandhi describes himself as 'a determined opponent of modern civilization',[23] he clearly has in mind the acquisitiveness and materialism of the West. This accounts for his expressed preference for the simple life and the pursuit of higher, spiritual ideals. There can be little doubt, however, that he resorts to sweeping generalizations when he proceeds to describe Western civilization as destructive, aimless, materialistic and activist, and Eastern civilization as constructive, purposeful, spiritual and contemplative.[24] He is also adopting an extreme position when he maintains that there can be a true meeting of East and West only when the West jettisons modern civilization.[25] He is less extreme when he acknowledges that it is possible for light to come from the West and that he himself might well profit from it provided he is not blinded by the glamour of the West.[26]

I have argued that Gandhi's educational concerns are rooted in his fundamental belief in the true nature of the Self, the essential unity of mankind and in the indivisibility of Truth. Sarvodaya was the natural consequence of his belief in the unity of mankind, and one of the ways in which the welfare of his fellow countrymen in particular could be served was by the provision of a suitable system of education that would cater for their needs. In Gandhi's view, the system of education that had been implemented by the British did not contribute to the welfare of the people of India or to their moral and spiritual well-being. Rather it served to alienate Indians from their own kith and kin and from their cultural heritage and created an educated élite without roots in the country of their birth. Such an educational policy was an intellectual and moral affront to the nation and a violation of the spirit of Truth. It undermined a man's knowledge of himself thereby creating a problem of identity.

It might be argued that Gandhi's alternative system of education could hardly be considered ideal. It could be criticized, for example, for being too vocationally oriented. Gandhi might well agree with this criticism, but that would not prevent him from maintaining it to be the better system in the circumstances. It was preferable to the system which simply produced a class of people sufficiently educated to take their place in the Indian civil service. Given the moral choice Gandhi would have no hesitation in choosing that system which, in his view, sought the welfare of the people of India, produced no crisis of self-identity, preserved the cultural heritage of the nation, and was not a violation of Truth as he conceived it.

Since it is not possible for an ideal system of education to be embodied in a particular empirical form it might be argued that he has to hold on to that system which approximates to the ideal. It is not that he is settling for less in the sense that he is dispensing with the ideal. The concept of the ideal still informs the way in which he looks at particular empirical systems in the same way as the concept of absolute Truth informs his choice of relative truths to be his beacon and guide. He proposes a system of education which he thinks meets the needs of the people of India and in so doing he acts in accordance with the religious and ethical ideals acquired within his own form of life and which he calls Truth.

NOTES TO CHAPTER VII

1 Selected Works, Vol. VI, p. 294; cf. *All Men are Brothers*, p. 156.
2 *All Men are Brothers*, p. 151.
3 Ibid., p. 157.
4 Ibid., p. 153.
5 *Selected Works*, Vol. VI, p. 521.
6 Ibid., p. 510.
7 *All Men are Brothers*, pp. 153–4.
8 Ibid., p. 154.
9 Ibid., p. 155.
10 This point has been developed admirably by J. R. Jones in his article 'How do I know who I am', *Aristotelean Society*, Vol. XLI, 1967, pp. 1–18, and I am indebted to his treatment of the subject.
11 The phrase has been used b John V. Canfield in an article on 'Wittgenstein and Zen', in *Philosophy*, (October, 1975), Vol. 50, No. 194.
12 *Philosophical Investigations*, (Blackwell, Oxford, 1976), p. 412.
13 *The Blue and Brown Books*, (Oxford, 1958), p. 68.
14 See my paper 'Conceptions of the Self in Wittgenstein, Hume and Buddhism: an Analysis and Comparison', *The Monist*, January, 1978. Vol. 61, No. I.
15 *Selections from Gandhi*, p. 284.
16 Ibid., pp. 284–5.
17 *The Essential Gandhi*, pp. 236–7.
18 Ibid., p. 299.
19 Ibid., p. 82.
20 *Selections from Gandhi*, p. 288.
21 *Selected Works*, Vol. VI, p. 519.
22 *The Essential Gandhi*, p. 238; *Selections from Gandhi*, p. 297; *Selected Works*, Vol. VI, p. 285.
23 *Selected Works*, Vol. VI, p. 276.
24 Ibid., pp. 279–81.
25 Ibid., p. 283.
26 Ibid., p. 286.

CHAPTER VIII

TRUTH AND ECONOMICS

Gandhi's theory of basic education and his plan to link the acquisitions of the skills of literary and numeracy with handicrafts like spinning and weaving, together with his stress on the importance of the vocational nature of higher education and the need for it to be economically self-sufficient, is a clear indication of the significance he attached to providing education with a sound economic basis. But he also conceived his theory of education to be 'the spearhead of a silent social revolution fraught with the most far-reaching consequences'.[1] The villages of India were in a state of progressive decay since they were regarded simply as appendages to the cities and fit only to be exploited. By relating vocational education to the requirements of the villages, Gandhi was setting in motion a programme of social reconstruction and laying the foundation for a more equitable social order. He was providing for a healthier relationship between city and village and for the elimination of some of the worst of the economic evils that had resulted from the exploitation of the villages.[2]

The close relation between Gandhi's theory of education and his social and economic views indicates the unitary nature of his teaching. The same point could be made in a different way. His conception of the indivisibility of Truth is related, as we have seen, to the idea of the oneness of mankind and the unity of all being. There may be many bodies but there is only one soul, for though the rays of the sun are many through refraction they have the same source. It follows that I am united with my fellow human beings. I cannot believe that God pervades everything in the universe without accepting both the unity of existence and the essential equality of all men. All men are brothers because they possess the same ātman or soul. Hence to exploit or injure another, as we have shown, is to do violence to oneself since the ātman is one and the same in all men.

The social and economic implications of Gandhi's metaphysical beliefs are far-reaching. We have already examined some of the social consequences of his views and we might look now at their economic implications. It is Gandhi's contention that no truly acceptable economic policy can ignore moral values. It should provide, for example, sufficient work for everyone to be able to feed and clothe himself and his family. The prodigality of nature is such that it produces more than enough for man's daily needs and provided everyone took just enough for himself there would be no poverty or starvation in the world.[3] If we were to maintain that this is too idealistic a solution of the world's inequalities, Gandhi's reply would be that although his ideal solution is equal distribution of the world's goods he would nevertheless be prepared to recognize that such an ideal is unrealizable, and to settle for equitable distribution.[4] This does not mean that he is settling for less in the sense that he is abandoning the ideal. Rather he is holding on to that which approximates to the ideal in the same way as he holds on to such relative truth as he is able to grasp since absolute Truth is empirically unattainable. In support of this aim he contends that should anyone seek to possess anything above and beyond his immediate needs, it could be construed as stolen property and indicative of lack of faith in the providence of God. The rich, he claims, have an overabundance of worldly goods while millions suffer want. It is the duty of the rich, therefore, to engage in dispossession and to dispose of a portion of their property thereby keeping their wealth within moderate limits, while at the same time creating a certain amount of happiness among the poor. Despite what he says about stolen property, however, Gandhi is sufficiently practical to realize that the rich could hardly be expected to relinquish all their wealth.

'Complete renunciation of one's possessions is a thing which very few even among ordinary folk are capable of. All that can legitimately be expected of the wealthy class is that they should hold their riches and talents in trust and use them for the service of the society. To insist on more would be to kill the goose that laid the golden eggs.'[5] It might be argued that this suggestion is as idealistic as the suggestion that there should be equal distribution of the world's goods and presupposes a highly optimistic view of human nature. The rich could not be forced to relinquish their surplus of the world's goods since that would involve himsā which would be contrary to Gandhian principles. They would have to be persuaded, according to Gandhi, to part voluntarily with their surplus wealth and riches.

The term that Gandhi uses to describe the voluntary sharing of riches is trusteeship. The essence of his doctrine of trusteeship is that a rich man should be allowed to retain his wealth and not be forcibly deprived of it. He should use it for whatever he reasonably requires to satisfy his personal needs and then act as trustee for the remainder of his wealth which should be used for the benefit of society as a whole. He is required to exercise self-restraint and to reduce his own needs to a minimum having regard for the extreme poverty of India and the fact that 3,000,000 people have to live on one inadequate meal a day.[6] According to Gandhi's teaching, therefore, equitable distribution of the wealth of a country is brought about by means of voluntary renunciation on the part of the rich. It could in fact be described as a voluntary form of socialism. The measure of altruism that the doctrine of trusteeship presupposes, however, ignores the basic acquisitiveness of human nature. This may well be the reason why so much ridicule was poured on the idea in the first place.[7] On the other hand it has to be acknowledged that some rich men, to some extent at least, have acted in accordance with Gandhi's teaching whether they were aware of it or not, and the names of Nuffield and Carnegie come to mind in this connection. It the rich could not be persuaded to act as trustees of their surplus wealth, then Gandhi advocates the use of non-violent non-cooperation and civil disobedience as the most effective means of removing social and economic inequalities.[8] He argues that since there can be no capitalists without workers, the workers have the means to become co-partners with the capitalists in the wealth produced and thereby free themselves from their economic poverty. A non-violent course of action, from a purely practical point of view alone, is preferable to the violent enforcement of egalitarianism which only succeeds in killing the goose that lays the golden eggs. But in any event violence is contrary to Gandhi's basic teaching and in his view the elimination of millionaires constitutes no solution to the problems of poverty and economic inequality.[9] If we were to maintain that non-violent non-cooperation in this context looks very much like the choice of a form of coercion since persuasion had failed, Gandhi might reply that this form of satyāgraha is simply another method of persuasion, which raises problems similar to those we have already discussed.

We have indicated that Gandhi was sufficiently practical to acknowledge that complete economic equality was beyond realization in the kind of social order he envisaged where ahiṁsā prevailed. He was in fact, unable to foresee a time when economic equality would prevail, but he claimed to be able to envisage a time when men would cease to enrich themselves at the expense of the poor. It is worth noting that Gandhi distinguishes between capitalism and capitalists. The latter, he maintains, are not necessarily exploiters; their interests are not really opposed to the interests of ordinary people. He objects to the unacceptable face of capitalism, or the wrong use of capital, rather than to capitalists as such.[10] This is consistent with his belief that the principle of ahiṁsā should apply to all living beings and his appeal to the wealthy on the one hand to exercise self-restraint, and the poor on the other hand to be non-violent in any campaign of non-cooperation they might engage in or undertake, is clearly derived from his basic beliefs in the unity of all being and the interrelation of all men as partakers of the same reality or Truth.

It is conceivable that Gandhi's appeal to the rich to hold their surplus wealth in trust for their less fortunate fellow human beings might be interpreted as a request for a greater display of charity and generosity on their part. This is far from being a correct interpretation, however, as Gandhi makes clear when he rejects sadā-vrata or donation, which involves the free gift of food to the poor. He is surely correct to regard the kind of charity whereby poor but healthy people are provided with free meals as shameful, degrading, and an encouragement to laziness, idleness, hypocrisy and crime.

'My *ahiṃsā* would not tolerate the idea of giving a free meal to a healthy person who has not worked for it in some honest way and if I had the power, I would stop every *sadāvrata* where free meals are given.'[11] This does not mean to say that charity is totally excluded. Two classes of people qualify for it, namely, the Brāhmana. who own nothing, and the cripple and blind. The State has an obligation and a duty to support the blind especially. But to dole out charity to healthy, able-bodied, poor people, is humiliating to both giver and receiver. The sight of beggars feeding in front of the majestic Marble Palace in Calcutta was not only incongruous but also exceedingly humiliating to Gandhi. Such charity was completely misplaced and simply served to give the rich donors a false sense of satisfaction.[12]

In place of sadāvrata Gandhi proposes the doctrine of bread labour. He first became aware of the concept on reading Tolstoy's views on the subject and prior to that Ruskin's *Unto This Last*. This is a further indication of his indebtedness to Tolstoy. Tolstoy had popularized T. M. Bondaref's theory that man must earn his bread by his own labour and Gandhi believed the same principle to be contained in the Gītā. But he also regarded it as common sense to maintain that man should, as the Bible states, eat his bread by the sweat of his brow. Although agriculture might well be considered the ideal way of implementing the concept of bread labour, it was not open to all to engage in agricultural activities. There was nothing, however, to prevent a man from spinning, weaving, taking up carpentry, or being his own scavenger and disposing of his own waste. Intellectual labour was not enough; it had an important place in the scheme of things but it did not do away with the need for manual labour.[13] In Gandhi's view the same principle applied to the saṃnyāsins. They ought not to feel that their spiritual teaching was sufficient in itself. They too were under an obligation to engage in manual labour. To do no work whatsoever was not an exercise in renunciation; it was rather an indication of inertia. Here Gandhi was clearly challenging cherished customs and beliefs and at the same time he was drawing a clear distinction between a saṃnyāsin and a vānaprasthin which is what he himself professed to be. He also challenged cherished beliefs when he rejected the traditional interpretation of the law of karma that attributed the pitiable condition of the starving poor to their actions in previous lives. By his actions Gandhi reinterpreted the law of karma and sought to undo the past by rearranging the present in accordance with the demands of mercy, pity and love.[14]

If it is argued that intellectual labour is on a par with manual labour since both engage in useful social work, Gandhi would reply that no man should consider himself to be free from the obligations of physical labour. In fact, physical labour might be considered a necessity in order to improve the quality of intellectual labour. What Gandhi is suggesting here is that sound educational practice, namely the combination of knowledge and handicrafts, or what Plato calls music and gymnastics, should also be regarded as sound social practice. He suggests that the intellectuals of ancient times, the brāhmans, readily engaged in manual labour as well as intellectual activity, so that the tendency of contemporary intellectuals to be slightly contemptuous of manual labour and to show a disinclination to soil their hands, was in marked contrast to ancient practice which supported the idea of the dignity of labour. Whether this is an accurate interpretation of ancient practice or not, it is clear that, as far as contemporary practice among the educated élite is concerned, Gandhi was proposing something quite revolutionary, since on the whole in India manual labour was regarded as the duty and prerogative of the lower stratas of society. His emphasis on bread labour, therefore, restores among other things the conception of the dignity of labour and the sacramental nature of work through which we identify ourselves with the poor and with the whole of mankind.[15]

The significance of Gandhi's doctrine of bread labour cannot be over-emphasized. He refers to it as having the potential to effect a silent revolution in the structure of society and the ability to revitalize village life.[16] His stress on the importance of the spinning wheel is related to the significance he attaches to bread labour. He sees it as a practical method of alleviating the wretchedness and misery of people brought about by famine and enforced idleness.

caused by alternating periods of drought and floods. The process of dehumanization that famine and idleness set in motion could only be resolved in the long run by flood prevention measures and the introduction of better methods of cultivation, but in the meantime how were the starving millions to be fed? Gandhi's answer is 'through the spinning wheel'.[17] Does this mean that Gandhi conceived of the spinning wheel as a temporary measure until such time as better methods of husbandry were introduced? Apparently not, for he claims that: 'No scheme of irrigation or other agricultural improvement that human ingenuity can conceive can deal with the vastly scattered population of India or provide work for the masses of mankind who are constantly thrown out of employment.'[18]

There was a time, according to Gandhi, when the people of India produced their own cloth in the same way as they produced their own food, but with the introduction of imported cloth from England and the construction of textile mills in India, home spinning and weaving tended to disappear. A two-fold loss had ensued: the loss of labour that went into the home production of clothes, and the loss of income required to purchase clothes from the mills. Gandhi's conclusion was that the revival of the cottage industry would go a long way to removing the poverty of the people.

'When once we have revived the one industry *(Khadi)* all other industries will follow. I would make the spinning wheel the foundation on which to build a sound village life; I would make the wheel the centre round which all other activities will revolve.'[19]

The Village Industries Association was an experiment in bread labour for Gandhi. The Charkhā, or Spinning-Wheel, was a symbol of self-help, freedom and national prosperity as well as a clear indication of the dignity of labour. He describes it as 'the symbol of non-violent economic self-sufficiency.'[20]

In addition to being a great social leveller in the sense that it removed the stigma attached to the idea of manual labour in the minds of the educated élite, it also served to restore the traditional village crafts, thereby promoting greater economic self-sufficiency and with it a greater measure of self-reliance and self-respect. The way in which Gandhi used the Charkhā as a symbol of India's desire for self-government and as a symbol of peace between Muslims and Hindus will be dealt with in connection with the political implications of his philosophy. Here we shall confine ourselves to examining further the economic implications of his teaching.

Arthur Koestler refers to the Charkhā as 'a symbol of the rejection of industrialization.'[21] This is a misleading though perfectly understandable statement. The misleading nature of this assessment of the significance of the Charkhā in Gandhi's thought is made clear by Gandhi's explicit statements on the subject. He maintains that hand-spinning is not meant to displace any existing form of industry nor to oust a man from any remunerative occupation that he might be engaged in. Its main purpose is 'to harness every single idle minute of our millions for common productive work.'[22] The cloth produced in the mills provided work for a limited number; home-spun cloth would give work to all. Gandhi uses a telling phrase in this context: 'Khadi serves the masses, mill cloth is intended to serve the classes. Khadi serves labour, mill cloth exploits it.'[23] It was because of the impoverishment of millions of Indian peasants resulting from the importation of cloth from England that Gandhi could refer to the practice as immoral. Mass-produced and highly-priced Lancashire textiles which had been dumped on the Indian market had, he claimed, reduced many of his fellow countrymen to pauperism. To wear khādī, therefore, was an expression of one's solidarity and kinship with one's neighbours. Gandhi refers to it as the spiritual aspect of the spinning-wheel and an expression or indication of one's sympathy with the poor. For this reason he advocated that the Congress party should make the wearing of khādī a condition of membership and make the daily use of the spinning-wheel a symbol of India's desire for self-determination and self-government. Khādī, in his view, connoted the start of economic freedom for India.[24]

Gandhi links the wearing of khādī to the concept of swadeshī which in this context he defines as the determination to find the necessities of life in India, and the use of home-produced goods to the exclusion of foreign-produced goods when the latter tended to undermine home industries and thereby impoverish the people of India. Khādī is in fact a corollary of the principle of swadeshī which involves the idea that one has a moral obligation to one's neighbour but does not, on that account, exclude the notion that one has a duty to all men. Swadeshī and sarvodaya are not mutually exclusive concepts in Gandhi's thought. As he explains, swadeshī does not mean the exclusion of all foreign goods from India no matter how beneficial they might be. To adopt such a policy would be to make a fetish of swadeshī and fetishes, as we have seen, are, in Gandhi's view, fit only to be discarded. Such a policy would also be totally contrary to the doctrine of ahiṁsā since it harbours ill-will and displays an antagonistic attitude to all things foreign. True swadeshī is that which serves the interests of the millions in India, and it is possible 'even though the capital and talent are foreign but under effective Indian control.'[25] On the other hand, it could be argued that although swadeshī and sarvodaya are not mutually exclusive in theory, it turns out that in practice the implementation of swadeshī did have an adverse effect on the lives of other human beings. For example, the boycott of imported cloth and its replacement by khādī produced much unemployment and distress in the Lancashire textile industry. Gandhi might well reply to this argument by maintaining that since the practice of importing British cloth was immoral in the first place and had resulted in the impoverishment of many Indians, it was only right and proper that it should be stopped. Furthermore, he might argue that his promotion of khādī and the swadeshī movement in general, was not motivated by any hatred of the textile workers of Lancashire or by any antagonism to foreign good as such. It was prompted rather by his concern for the poverty, suffering and distress of many of his fellow countrymen, who were his nearest neighbours. By serving them he was serving God and pursuing Truth to the best of ability. But it has to be recognized that here Gandhi is confronted by the same kind of moral dilemma that we have referred to previously in other connections. On the one hand, he cherishes the ideal that one has a duty to promote the best interest of humanity as a whole and, on the other hand, he acknowledges that he has a moral obligation to serve the interests of his fellow countrymen. Although the implementation of swadeshī adversely affected the lives of Lancashire cotton-mill workers, Gandhi would still maintain that it was the right course of action for him to take in the circumstances and that he had not thereby relinquished the ideal of sarvodaya.

Gandhi speaks of swadeshī as 'ingrained in the basic nature of man' and in its spiritual sense as standing for 'the final emancipation of the soul from her earthly bondage.'[26] But what does he mean by this statement? If we were to adopt the same philosophical approach to this remark as we applied to the question of personal identity in the previous chapter, we might explain it by maintaining that we know ourselves as members of a human community which is bound together by the same language, customs and traditions, and that swadeshī refers to our deep concern for that community apart from which we do not know in any real sense who we are. While Gandhi might accept this explanation as an interpretation of the way we know ourselves, he would also maintain that self-knowledge is knowledge of Truth or God and that swadeshī is an indication of our concern for, and dedication to, the service of our fellow countrymen, our immediate neighbours. It is through the service of his neighbours that a man comes to know the Truth, and knowledge of Truth or God is self-knowledge, which in turn is mokṣa, or the emancipation of the soul from the saṁsāric realm. That is, Gandhi conceives man's duty or svadharma, in the sense in which the Gītā describes it, to be related to his immediate environment and his immediate neighbours.[27]

The controversial nature of Gandhi's emphasis on khādī is evident not only from Koestler's misleading interpretation of the significance of the Charkhā, but also from the accusation levelled against him that he was leading the country back into the dark ages. Gandhi's defence is that he is seeking to make 7,000,000 villages in India self-sufficient units rather than the exploited source of the wealth of cities in India and Britain. He does not mean by this that he is seeking to make the villages totally self-contained units. They should be self-sufficient with regard to the basic necessities of life, but since it is not possible for the villages to produce all their needs, they should produce enough of what they are best able to produce in order to exchange it for what they cannot produce.[28] The spinning-wheel could possibly be considered mediaeval, but whereas it was once a symbol of slavery it was now, in Gandhi's view, a symbol of freedom, unity and equality. The restoration of the village industry meant the return of life to the villages.

What the khādī scheme involved was the decentralization of the means of production and distribution of one of life's necessities. This in turn implied the decentralization of the cultivation and processing of cotton. Did this mean that Gandhi favoured the decentralization of all industries and that the spinning-wheel was after all, to use Koestler's phrase, 'a symbol of the rejection of industrialization' as it is normally understood? The answer to the first part of the question is that Gandhi did not envisage the decentralization of all industries. He maintains: 'Heavy industries will needs be centralized and nationalized. But they will occupy the least part of the vast national activity which will mainly be in the villages.'[29] In answer to the second part of the question, it would be misleading to suggest that Gandhi is opposed to industrialization as such. If by industrialization we mean the introduction of machinery that would help to remove the poverty of India and at the same time avoid the creation of unemployment among the masses, then Gandhi would most certainly be in favour of it. He is not opposed to the introduction of machinery provided it does not displace human labour and result in the tragedy of enforced idleness.

'Machinery has its place; it has come to stay. But it must not be allowed to displace the necessary human labour... I would favour the use of the most elaborate machinery if thereby India's pauperism and resulting idleness be avoided.'[30] Machines that lighten the burden of millions then are welcome, but labour-saving machines that put thousands out of work are rejected. Gandhi sees the primary motivation for the introduction of such machines to be greed on the part of the privileged few rather than an act of philanthropy. If we were to argue that the creation of wealth by means of mass production is bound to increase the wealth of the country as a whole and ultimately benefit everyone, Gandhi's reply might well be that enforced idleness and mass unemployment is unlikely to benefit anyone in the long run, no matter how great an increase there might be in the standard of living.

Clearly Gandhi is opposed to the abuses of industrialization rather than the concept of industrialization and he seeks to limit not eradicate the use of machines. He refuses to be blinded by the magnificence of machines. Under no circumstances should they be allowed to deprive a man of his right to work. The kind of machine Gandhi favours is the one which saves a person from unnecessary labour, and the sewing-machine is cited as a perfect example. It may be argued that the production of such a machine requires heavy industry of the centralized type that Gandhi does not want to see multiplied indiscriminately. While this is undoubtedly the case, and readily admitted by Gandhi, he insists that, like all other heavy centralized industries, it should be nationalized and run for the benefit of humanity as a whole. This would involve the provision of ideal working conditions and the replacement of the profit motive by humanitarian considerations. In short, what Gandhi is advocating is a proper philosophy of work which neither degrades nor dehumanizes people and which shows concern for the quality of life of ordinary people. It will be seen that this philosophy is consistent with his teaching concerning the oneness of humanity and the unity of life.

It may be argued that the decentralization of the processing of cotton through the introduction of the khādī programme spelt the end and virtual destruction of the textile industry in India. Gandhi maintains that this is not his intention and that he wants the textile industry to succeed. Yet at the same time he can refer to the cotton-mill industry as one that 'exploits the masses and deepens their poverty in exact proportion to its success over Khadi',[31] and that should the interests of the country demand it he would permit the mill industry to die without hesitation. It is difficult to reconcile his desire to see the industry succeed with his description of it as profit-motivated and as exploiting the masses. Perhaps what he wants is for it to succeed in a new guise, that is, to operate as a nationalized industry for the benefit of society as a whole. Though whether one can speak meaningfully of the good of society as a whole is another question.

We have seen that Gandhi is not opposed to the kind of industrialization that alleviates the poverty, idleness and misery of the masses in India. He is, however, totally opposed to that kind of industrialization whereby the mass production of goods is controlled by a small number of people with the aid of sophisticated machinery. That is, he rejects industrialization which 'concentrated power in the hands of the few who amassed fortunes at the expense of the many.'[32] He considers it, in fact, to be the curse of mankind depending as it does on the ability of producers to exploit world markets, which, if they fail to do so, results in increased unemployment in the industrial countries concerned. Because of its essentially competitive nature Gandhi firmly believed the future of industrialism to be dark. The West had, in his view, already seen enough of industrialization and exploitation and since that was the case it could hardly be regarded as a panacea for the ills of India.[33] Industrial communities needed to be able to exploit world markets. They were not primarily concerned with the possible adverse social consequences of their methods of exploitation. This was the reason why Gandhi found himself totally opposed to this form of industrialization and dedicated to bringing about its ultimate destruction.[34] In the sense in which Koestler used the term then the spinning-wheel could be rightly regarded as 'a symbol of the rejection of industrialization'. What is misleading about the statement is that it does not allow for the possibility of conceiving a different and, from Gandhi's standpoint at least, a more acceptable form of industrialization where people mattered.

The question that needs to be asked at this point is whether the alternative form of industrialization suggested by Gandhi is in any way a viable option in the modern world. Some light may be shed on this question by a consideration of the economic theory propounded by E. F. Schumacher, the author of *Small is Beautiful* and founder of the Intermediate Technology Development Group with its Indian counterpart the Appropriate Technology Development Association.[35] The sub-title of Schumacher's book namely, 'Economics as if People Mattered', is significant, and a clear indication that his approach to economics is basically similar to that of Gandhi. In his introduction to this work, Theodore Roszak notes that the first example of Schumacher's work he had come across was a talk 'on the practicality of Gandhi's economic program in India' delivered in the 1960s, in which Schumacher commented on the essential good sense of the economic policy of the Third World that rejected the Western model of centralized industries, mass production and urbanization. Schumacher took Gandhi's economic principles seriously, despite their lack of professionalism and sophistication, because, in his view, they indicated a wise soul deeply concerned with the quality of life of ordinary people. He approved of Gandhi's quest for methods and machines sufficiently cheap to be made available to everyone and at the same time suitable to be applied on a small scale and consistent with the creative needs of man.[36] He recognized also that the wisdom required to be able to free oneself from the greed that had made man captive to the power of the machine in the first place, could only come from acknowledging with Gandhi that man possessed a soul as well as a body.[37]

Schumacher's thesis is based on his conception of the role of economics. He maintains that the judgments of economics are essentially fragmentary, for, when an activity is described as uneconomic what it means is that it does not earn a profit for those who undertake it. But that judgment fails to take into consideration the social, aesthetic or moral values of the activity concerned, hence its fragmentary nature. The limitations of the role of economics, however, are not always recognized, and Schumacher rightly insists that it is the duty of economists 'to understand and clarify its limitations, that is to say, to understand meta-economics.'[38] What he means by this is that it is essential for the economist to recognize the 'derived' nature of his thinking. He needs to understand that his aims and objectives are derived from certain basic presuppositions concerning the nature of man, and that his methods derive from presuppositions concerning nature. When his view of man and nature changes, so do his economic judgments. Although Gandhi never expresses himself in quite these terms, it is clear that his attitude to the economics of industrialization is profoundly influenced by his metaphysical presuppositions concerning the nature of man and God or Truth. To use Schumacher's terminology, his people-oriented economic theory is derived from his understanding of meta-economics. He is less concerned with the material benefits that might accrue from mass production technology than he is with the adverse social consequences of the methods of mass production. This is not to imply that he is opposed to improving the lot of the masses in India. On the contrary, his dedication to sarvodaya and swadeshī clearly indicates his sympathy and concern for the welfare of his fellow countrymen. What he is opposed to is the kind of economic development that ignores creative activity, undermines social structures, and imperils the spiritual well-being of his felow man. It was his understanding of Truth and the nature of man tlhat determined his attitude to industrialization.

Schumacher illustrated his thesis by means of an examination of Buddhist economics though, as he points out, the teaching of any Eastern or Western religion would apply equally well. What he suggests is that a religious view of man and nature is likely to affect one's economic judgments. The fourth noble truth of Buddhism is the eightfold path. This is the path one takes in order to remove craving (tānhā) that binds one to the saṁsāric world of suffering (duḥkha). One of the requirements of the eightfold path is right livelihood which, as Schumacher points out, involves economics. In Buddhist thought then, it is not possible for economic judgments to conflict with religious values. That is to say, a Buddhist way of life demands Buddhist economics. The Buddhist philosophy of work, according to Schumacher, is that a man should develop his own talents, and seek to remove the self-centredness which perpetuates his craving and binds him to the world of suffering. He should do this by participating with others in the common task necessary to produce goods for a world in a state of becoming and characterized by impermanence (anicca).[39] Because it lays more stress on the development of character than on the production of goods, Buddhist economics would not find the economics of modern materialism in any way acceptable; the meta-economics of the one differs from that of the other. Gandhi's philosophy of work is similar to that of Buddhism. As we have seen, he links swadeshī to his dedication to the service of his immediate neighbours, and it is through such service that he comes to know Truth or God. The meta-economics of both Gandhi and Buddhism is totally opposed to the meta-economics of materialism that would, in Schumacher's words, consider 'goods as more important than people and consumption as more important than creative activity. It means shifting the emphasis from the worker to the product of work, that is, from the human to the sub-human, a surrender to the forces of evil.'[40]

The similarity between Buddhist economics and Gandhian principles is further illustrated by the common view that the most rational approach to rural life is that which seeks to create self-sufficient economic units of all local communities with the necessities of life being produced from local resources. According to Schumacher, the Buddhist economist would consider it a failure if he had to import goods in order to satisfy basic local needs. The economics of modern materialism has no such aim. It is not basically concerned with the social or spiritual values of community life and such considerations do not normally enter into its assessments. It is not altogether surprising, therefore, that the modern economic approach with its materialistic outlook should have resulted in the collapse of the village economy, the growth of rural unemployment and the creation of a city proletariat.[41] Schumacher is at one with Gandhi in his rejection of the kind of industrialization and economic progress that has produced such disastrous results.

But the question is whether the alternative form of industrialization proposed by Gandhi is a practical proposition. Schumacher seems to think that it is. He approves of Gandhi's suggestion that what is needed is production by the masses and not mass production. Gandhi was convinced that the mania for mass production was responsible for much of the exploitation of the poorer countries by the wealthy industrial nations. Schumacher supports Gandhi's arguments and goes further in his condemnation of modern technology when he maintains: 'The technology of *mass production* is inherently violent, ecologically damaging, self-defeating in terms of

non-renewable resources, and stultifying for the human person.'[42]
Production by the masses on the other hand, as Schumacher shows,
is localized, ecologically sound, careful in its use of natural resources, and essentially humane. It is more concerned with people than
with goods and encourages creativity rather than consumption.
The name Schumacher gives to the technology of production by the
masses is intermediate technology, or as it is called in India, appropriate technology. He describes it also as self-help technology or
people's technology. His contention is that it is precisely the kind
of technology needed in the Third World since the poverty of those
countries, fortunately, made the adoption of Western technology
with its high capital expenditure almost impossible. The Third
World was fortunate, in Schumacher's view, because it could be
spared the problems of unemployment and rural depopulation that
had characterized industrial development and the technology of
mass production in the West. His argument is that the need of the
Third World is also the pressing need of the West, namely, a return
to simplicity and directness rather than a forward stampede in the
direction of greater sophistication and complexity.[43]

We may ask whether this is not a regressive rather than a progressive policy. Can it possibly be maintained that we believe in
progress if a less sophisticated and simpler form of technology is
adopted? In other words, is this alternative form of industrialization
a practical proposition? Schumacher's reply is that it depends entirely on what is meant by progress. If increased sophistication and
complexity in technological development constitutes progress, then
it would have to be admitted that intermediate or appropriate
technology could not be regarded as progressive. If, however,
increased care in the use of natural resources, concern for the
environment, and the encouragement of creativity and the maximum
use of labour is progress, then intermediate technology, or production by the masses, as Gandhi calls it, can be classified as progressive.
Schumacher's view is that the technology both he and Gandhi pro-
pose, namely, technology with a human face, is both viable and
practical, but he recognizes that 'to redirect technology so that it
serves man instead of destroying him requires primarily an effort

of the imagination and an abandonment of fear.'[44] Schumacher does
not suggest, any more than Gandhi does, that the developing countries can do without a modern sector, or some form of heavy centralized industry. But, like Gandhi, he does not envisage it occupying
or absorbing the total activity of both the urban and rural population of the countries of the Third World. This applies particularly
where developing countries are in direct contact with rich countries.
It applies also to the production of those types of commodities
where heavy centralized industry is essential and for Gandhi the
sewing-machine would be a case in point.[45]

Among the reasons Schumacher gives for the viability and
practicality of intermediate technology is that it provides help for
those who need it most by means of relatively simple equipment
which could be used by the most unsophisticated persons after a
minimum amount of training. The highest percentage of the people
of the developing countries live in small towns and villages. It
would be of little help to them to establish big industries in the
cities, for that would simply encourage migration from the villages
and towns to the cities thereby creating further problems associated
with social upheaval, rural depopulation and urban unemployment.
The need was to establish an 'agro-industrial structure' in the villages and small towns, which would involve innumerable places of
work providing the maximum number of job opportunities. This
was Gandhi's argument also, and his promotion of the spinning-
wheel with its accompanying khādī programme was directed
specifically towards that end. It provided help for those who needed
it most. Both Gandhi and Schumacher, therefore, saw the need for
a decentralized approach to economic development in the Third
World and both were prompted by humanitarian considerations
derived from fundamental metaphysical presuppositions.

It is possible to describe Schumacher and Gandhi's approach to
economic development as labour-intensive as opposed to the cap-
ital-intensive approach of modern mass-production technology.
But to draw such a distinction would be misleading. The appro-
priateness of intermediate technology to an industrial project would
undoubtedly have in mind the distinction between labour-intensity

and capital-intensity but that would not be its initial point of departure. The kind of question that might be asked at the outset would be: what is the most appropriate technology to be used in this particular situation? As Schumacher maintains: 'In the end, intermediate technology will be "labour-intensive" and will lend itself to use in small-scale establishments. But neither "labour-intensity" nor "small-scale" implies "intermediate technology".'[46]

If it is objected that intermediate technology or production by the masses really means settling for second best, Schumacher's reply is that when a person is face to face with starvation he is primarily concerned with the means of subsistence and not with what is best or second best. If it is further argued that the quickest rate of economic growth is obtained by the use of modern sophisticated machinery rather than the simple unsophisticated machinery of intermediate technology, Schumacher replies that 'it is wrong to assume that the most sophisticated equipment, transplanted into an unsophisticated environment, will be regularly worked at full capacity'.[47] That is to say, the argument fails to take into account 'the dynamic approach to development, which treats the choice of appropriate, intermediate technologies as the central issue...'[48]

Both Gandhi and Schumacher, as we have seen, admit that there is need of sophisticated machinery to produce some products, but both insist on the need for less sophisticated environments. The question is whether intermediate technology is at all possible without modern sophisticated technology to back it up. In reply to this, Schumacher maintains that it would be a mistake to assume that the scientific achievements of the West are necessarily embedded in highly sophisticated machinery. We cannot equate man's scientific achievements with sophisticated machinery which after all is simply the product of his scientific achievements. What is being suggested is that it is the technological expertise which is important not the machinery, and that technical expertise can be applied in a variety of different ways. Intermediate technology is the application of technological knowledge to particular situations for the realization of specific ends. It could well involve the transformation of advanced techniques and traditional technology in order that in

specific cases the desired goals might be achieved.[49] Schumacher
emphasizes the importance of the right choice of technology. The
more sophisticated the technology the greater will be the requirements by way of capital, machinery and skilled labour. Such sophisticated machinery is hardly necessary, however, to produce the
simple necessities of life in developing countries and it is a mistake
to assume that no other choice exists. One of the main aims of the
Intermediate Technology Development Group is to discover what
the technological choices are in specific situations. By so doing it
is not turning the clock back, or implementing out-dated methods;
it is applying appropriate technology to meet the needs of people in
order to help them to help themselves; it is providing the relevant
expertise and experience to enable people to become self-supporting, self-reliant and independent.[50]

It is clear that both Gandhi and Schumacher are proposing an
economic theory that is oriented towards people. The alternative
forms of industrialization they suggest are basically similar and
spring from similar fundamental metaphysical presuppositions. In
Gandhi's case his economic policy derives from his quest for Truth
or God. No form of industrial development can be tolerated which
dehumanizes or degrades the lives of people and adds to their misery. That would consistitue a form of hiṁsā and would be contrary to the Truth.

'Economics that hurts the moral well-being of an individual or
nation is immoral and, therefore, sinful... True economics never
militates against the highest ethical standard, just as all true ethics
to be worth its name must at the same time be also good economics.'[51] On the other hand, to serve one's fellow man by the introduction of the right kind of industrial development that nourishes
rather than destroys existing communities is a form of ahiṁsā and
consistent with the Truth.

What emerges from this examination of the economic implications of Gandhi's teaching is the way in which the ethical and religious ideals acquired within his own form of life, and which he
calls Truth, dominate his outlook. His experiments with Truth in
the economic sphere meant that where, in his view, economic poli-

cies militated against ethical standards and undermined the moral well-being of individuals and the welfare of the people as a whole they should be discarded. His approach to economics is people-oriented; it is economics as if people mattered. It might be argued by protagonists of a consumer-oriented, mass-production techno-logy, that since the material wealth of a nation is increased overall by means of this kind of economic programme, the welfare of the people is being adequately provided for. The well-being of indi-viduals is not automatically undermined by methods of mass-production. Might it not be considered too simplistic an approach to economics to suggest that on the one hand we have the non-creative, consumer-oriented mentality of mass-production technol-ogy and, on the other hand, the productive activity of appropriate technology providing scope for individual creativity? Gandhi might acknowledge the simplistic nature of this distinction but, like Schumacher, he would still want to insist on the many problems mass-production technology creates in countries like India with its increasing population and immense resources of labour. He might want to argue that it would be better for people to be engaged on simple tasks, however menial, than that they should be thrown on the scrapheap of industrial unemployment. It would be better still in a labour intensive country if many could perform creative, self-satisfying tasks in a variety of small, unsophisticated, decentralized 'cottage' industries, than that a few should be employed in highly centralized industries with sophisticated machinery. The former economic policy would be more likely to provide for the welfare of the people and their moral well-being. It may not be possible for an ideal economic system to be embodied in a particular empirical form, but this does not mean that one settles for less in the sense that the ideal is discarded. The ideal still informs the way in which one examines particular economic systems in the same way as the concept of absolute Truth informs our choice of relative truths to be our guide. Gandhi proposes an economic system that, in his view, approximates to the ideal and is in accord with the principle of sarvodaya and the spirit of Truth.

NOTES TO CHAPTER VIII

1   *Selected Works*, Vol. VI, p. 512.
2   Ibid., p. 511–2.
3   Ibid,. p. 325; cf. *All Men are Brothers*, p. 130.
4   *All Men are Brothers*, p. 129.
5   Ibid,. p. 137.
6   Ibid., p. 132.
7   Ibid., p. 131.
8   Ibid., p. 132.
9   Ibid., p. 135; cf. *Selections from Gandhi*, pp. 78–9.
10 Ibid., p. 136; cf. *Selected Works*, Vol. VI, p. 339.
11 Ibid., p. 134; cf. *Selected Works*, Vol. VI, p. 334.
12 *Selections from Gandhi*, p. 47; cf. *The Essential Gandhi*, p. 230.
13 Ibid., pp. 51–4, cf. *Selected Works*, Vol. VI, p. 332.
14 *Selected Works*, Vol. V, p. 404; cf. *In Search of the Supreme*, Vol. 2, p. 125.
15 *Selections from Gandhi*, p. 50.
16 Ibid., p. 52.
17 Ibid., p. 55.
18 Ibid., p. 56.
19 *Selected Works*, Vol. VI, p. 393.
20 Ibid.
21 'The Yogi and the Commissar', *New York Times Magazine*, 5 Oct. 1969.
22 *Selections from Gandhi*, p. 57.
23 Ibid., p. 58.
24 Ibid., p. 59; cf. *Selected Works*, Vol. VI, p. 385.
25 *Selections from Gandhi*, p. 307.
26 *Selected Works*, Vol. IV, p. 256.
27 Ibid., p. 257.
28 *Selected Works*, Vol. VI, p. 350.
29 *Selected Works*, Vol. IV, p. 346.
30 *Selected Works*, Vol. VI, pp. 379–80.
31 *Selections from Gandhi*, p. 68.
32 Ibid., p. 71.
33 *Selected Works*, Vol. VI, pp. 276–8.
34 *Selections from Gandhi*, pp. 63–4.
35 The headquarters of this movement in India is located significantly enough in the Gandhi Bhavan at Lucknow. I discussed the aims and objectives of the movement with M. M. Hoda the executive director of the movement and editor of the news letter *Op. tech.*, and with M. K. Garg, the director of projects. Present at the discussion also was Mark Sinclair from the London headquarters of the Intermediate Technology Development Group. The close similarity between Gandhi's aims for the revival of the village industries and the aims of the Intermediate and

Appropriate Technology movements justifies, in my view, an examination of the basic economic theory of their founder E. F. Schumacher.

36   *Small is Beautiful*, (Harper & Row, New York, 1973), p. 32.
37   Ibid., pp. 36–7.
38   Ibid., p. 44.
39   Ibid., p. 51. Schumacher's article on Buddhist Economics first appeared in *Asia: A Handbook*, edited by Guy Wint. (Anthony Blond Ltd., London, 1966).
40   Ibid., p. 53.
41   Ibid., p. 58.
42   Ibid., p. 145.
43   Ibid., pp. 145–6.
44   Ibid., p. 151.
45   Ibid., p. 158; cf. *Selected Works*, Vol. IV, p. 346.
46   Ibid., pp. 168–9.
47   Ibid., p. 172.
48   Ibid., p. 173–4.
49   Ibid., pp. 176–7.
50   Ibid., pp. 201–2.
51   *Selected Works*, Vol. VI, pp. 321–2.

CHAPTER IX

TRUTH AND POLITICS

Gandhi's concept of Truth or God, as we have seen, led him to realize the importance of ahimsā as the means for the attainment of Truth, and action in the service of others as the way to its realization. Through the service of humanity and action in the cause of brotherhood, men came to a better understanding and a more complete realization of the nature of Truth or God. All men are united in the common bond of humanity and though there are many bodies there is but one soul. Such is the oneness or unitary nature of human existence, in Gandhi's view, that we do not exploit others without hurting ourselves ultimately. The implications of these metaphysical beliefs are far-reaching. Hitherto we have examined their social and economic significance; it is necessary now to look at some of their political consequences.

The importance Gandhi attaches to politics is made clear by the way he refuses to draw a distinction between religion and politics. For him religion is not just one aspect of a man's life or one of the many activities he engages in. To talk of leaving religion for politics or politics for religion was incomprehensible to him for he conceived of every activity as determined or governed by one's religious outlook.[1] Religion for him meant participating in politics. Far from advocating that religion should be kept out of politics, he insists that to be truly religious means taking an active part in political life. This is hardly the kind of attitude that one would expect of a samnyāsin within the orthodox Hindu tradition, whose negative attitude to empirical existence would preclude the possibility of his participating in politics. It might be argued that it is not the kind of attitude that would normally be expected of a vānaprasthin either, for to some extent he too withdraws from some of the normal obligations of life in society. It that is so, and if Gandhi insists on regarding himself as a vānaprasthin then it can only mean that he was giving the term a different connotation from that found in the classical,

Hindu tradition. He actively participated in every aspect of life consistent with his brahmacārya vow and viewed life with all its activities as an indivisible whole. He insists that it is not possible to divide social, economic, political and purely religious work into watertight compartments.[2] Religion, for him, involved all forms of human activity and at the same time provided it with a moral foundation.

At one time Gandhi was described as having the reputation of a saint and yet letting his political instincts determine his decisions and actions. His response to this was to reject the appellation saint as being too sacred a word to be applied to a simple searcher after truth like himself. He also rejected the suggestion that he was basically a politician, though he admitted to introducing religion into politics in the sense that he always acted from religious motives.[3] Clearly his metaphysical presuppositions determined his conviction that religion should pervade all our actions, and by religion he means, as we have noted, not a specific religion like Hinduism, Islam or Christianity, but that which transcends particular religions yet does not displace them, or that which 'harmonises them and gives them reality'.[4]

Gandhi firmly believed that he could not live a truly religious life unless he took part in political activity, but at the same time he was convinced that politics bereft of religion was of little value. It is as if he is claiming that great importance has to be attached to man's motivation for participating in political activity. That is, a metapolitics that considers personal aggrandisment and self-interest as significant and important would be diametrically opposed to the metapolitics of Gandhi which could be described as a people-oriented politics, or politics where people matter. Since political activity, in Gandhi's view, should be concerned with the welfare of men and nations it is essential that it should be permeated by religion and at least be the basic concern of people who are religiously motivated.[5] Politics permeated by religion, therefore, means politics dedicated to serve the needs of humanity and such service leads inevitably to a better understanding of Truth. For Gandhi, therefore, the Kingdom of heaven is not an eschatological event to be experienced in some kind of post-mortem existence. If we were to express his views in Western theological terms we would say that he is a firm believer in realized eschatology. The Kingdom of God is here and now and is established through political activity in the service of humanity.[6]

Gandhi would have sympathized with and approved of the struggle for human rights. He supports and defends the rights of the individual and agrees with Thoreau that the government which governs least is best.The growth of the power of the state and its encroachment on individual freedom is a matter of deep concern to him. The good that it does in preventing the exploitation of the people is counterbalanced by the harm it does by undermining individual freedom and initiative. His concern for individual liberty is such that he thinks we should be prepared to die rather than live in slavery, and his lifelong struggle for self-government in India seems to bear out his passionate belief in the value and importance of freedom. It may well be that many who have engaged in a continuous struggle against different forms of colonialism or totalitarianism during the course of history would be prepared to share his views.

His stress on individual freedom, however, does not imply that he failed to recognize the need for some form of social restraint. If we are to avoid anarchy we have to recognize that man is a social being and that individual liberty without laws to regulate it degenerates into licence. What is required, according to Gandhi, is voluntary acceptance of social restraints for the benefit of society as a whole. Every individual should be able to use whatever talents he has to the full, but this is only possible when he uses them in a way which is consistent with the demands or rules of the society to which he belongs. Individual liberty is preserved when a man voluntarily accepts social obligations; it is destroyed when he is forced to act against his will and contrary to his deepest convictions.[7]

In spite of his recognition of the need to accept social restraints Gandhi is able to refer to what he calls enlightened anarchy. What he means by this is that in an enlightened state everyone is his own ruler. 'He rules himself in such a manner that he is never a hindrance to his neighbour.'[8] What this amounts to in effect is an acceptance of the fact that one cannot live in a society without accepting voluntarily the need to curb one's activities or, in other words, the need for social restraints. Enlightened anarchy is simply another way of expressing the individual's free acceptance of his social obligations. In an ideal society individuals would not need to be restrained by social laws because life would be self-regulated, but since the ideal is beyond realization in practice, laws are necessary in order that men might live together in society.

Gandhi seems to be suggesting here that the laws of society are a necessary evil and that in an ideal society man would be sufficiently enlightened to regulate himself without the need of social laws. But are social laws necessarily opposed to individual freedom? A different view would be that social laws and the exercise of political authority by the State is not necessarily an affront to human freedom and rationality.[9] Peter Winch points out correctly that the anarchist reaction to social restraints is 'to reject as contrary to man's dignity as a rational being the whole social structure which brings one man under the authority of another in a way which does not depend on the free, rationally given, consent of the one who is subservient.'[10] This would seem to be a clear expression and an accurate assessment of Gandhi's state of enlightened anarchy. The question that arises is whether it is possible to understand what it might mean to be a free, rational being, independent of 'particular forms of social life within which rationality is exercised'.[11] Winch's argument is that authority exercised through social laws is not necessarily an infringement of individual freedom. The concepts of 'authority' and 'rationality' are not necessarily opposed to one another. Man's freedom can be infringed by the exercise of state authority of course, but particular cases of infringement of individual freedom by the State do not justify drawing the conclusion that 'authority' and 'rationality' are necessarily opposed to one another. As Winch points out, 'authority' and 'rationality' are 'concepts which have complex and shifting relations to each other depending on the contexts within which they are being applied'.[12]

Self-regulation or self-rule is the definition Gandhi gives to the sacred Vedic term Swarāj. There is a sense in which Swarāj indicates what he means by enlightened anarchy but whereas enlightened anarchy applies to an individual's ability to manage his own affairs, Swarāj refers to a nation's ability to manage its own affairs. It involves the government of India by the consent of the people of India. Gandhi's view is that every country has the right to govern itself. It may do so rather indifferently but no matter how badly it manages its own affairs, the fact remains that good government by others is no substitute for self-government. No self-respecting race of people can possibly appreciate being in a constant state of servitude and subjection. Self-government then is a matter of self-respect; it involves the will and determination to strive against odds to solve one's own problems and, as Gandhi shows, it is not unrelated to individual self-control and the acceptance of social obligations.

'*Swaraj* of a people means the sum total of the Swaraj (self-rule) of individuals. And such *Swaraj* comes only from performance by individuals of their duty as citizens.'[13] The implication of this description is that political self-determination is achieved in exactly the same way as individual self-regulation. That is, national rights are an extension of individual human rights. As an individual should regulate his activities so as not to encroach upon his neighbour's rights even so a nation should govern itself in such a way as not to usurp the rights of any other nation. The legal maxim: *Sic utere tuo ut alienum non laedas* (Use your own rights in such a way that you do not harm those of others), has a moral foundation and is consistent with the principle of ahimsā. The nation that acquires Swarāj, therefore, as Gandhi understands the term, can never prove a menace to the rights of the individuals of which it is comprised, nor to the rights of other nations, for it is grounded in Truth and ahimsā.

It is on account of his overriding concern for the rights of all individuals and all communities that Gandhi refers to the Swarāj of his dream as Pūrṇa Swarāj. It is pūrṇa, or complete, because it applies to all individuals irrespective of their race, religion or social status; it is as much the possession of the Muslim as the Hindu, the prince as the peasant.

'The very connotation of the word and the means of its attainment to which we are pledged, — Truth and Non-violence — precludes all possibility of that *Swaraj* being more for some one than for the other, being partial to some one and prejudicial to the other ... *Swaraj* under this method, therefore, can never be achieved by usurping the rights of any community, big or small, but by ensuring even-handed justice and fair treatment to all —even the poorest and the weakest in the land.'[14]

It is pūrṇa also because it means that all members of the community are ensured full rights. There can be no favoured treatment of one section of the community to the detriment of another section. There can be no unholy alliance with vested interests for the exploitation of the masses. This is what Gandhi means by true democracy for it provides the same opportunity for the weak as for the strong and preserves individual freedom for all by non-violent means. There can be no true democracy, for instance, where all opposition is forcibly removed and individual liberty is suppressed. And what applies within nations also applies between nations. A self-governing India would not constitute a threat to the other nations of the world. No exploitation of other weaker nations could be tolerated for Swarāj would involve India in the service of humanity and in an obligation to work for the good of all.[15]

The difficulty posed here by Gandhi's views on Pūrṇa Swarāj is whether one can legitimately speak of the interests or good of society as a whole. Can it be assumed that there is such a thing as the general interest or the general good of society? Does not the good of society correspond to what the person who talks about it thinks would be best for everyone? Rush Rhees underlines the difficulty of speaking about the general interest of society *vis-à-vis* the selfish interests of individuals when he states that what actually happens in society is that people press sectional interests not against the general interest of society but against the interests of those with opposing views. Society consists of people with conflicting interests hence the difficulty of speaking legitimately of the interest of society, or the national interest, as if it were clear what was meant by the use of these terms.[16]

From what has been said hitherto it can be deduced that Gandhi did not consider nationalistic aspirations to be in any way unjustified. On the contrary he regarded the desire for national self-determination to be an extension of the need to ensure basic human rights. If the latter is a matter of deep concern then the former cannot possibly be ignored for to be prevented from governing one's own affairs is to be deprived of one's basic rights. The end, Swarāj, is attained by means of Truth and non-violence and since means and ends are convertible terms according to Gandhi, it follows that Swarāj must be grounded in Truth and ahimsā. This might be expressed theologically by saying that national self-determination is the will of God. We have already shown how important and significant Gandhi felt the traditions, language and cultural heritage of a country to be to those who belong to it, and how strongly he resisted the forces that tended to undermine them in India, namely, the educational policy of the British and the missionary activity of certain Christian sects. To undermine the culture of a country by demeaning its language and debasing its traditions is to deprive a man of his roots in his native soil and to take away his self-respect. It could be argued from the particular modern philosophic standpoint we have already referred to that it also deprives him of self-identity. As we have shown, for an individual to know who he is he must be able for the benefit of others to pick himself out from among his neighbours, that is, from other people similar to himself. The individual is not logically independent of his environment; on the contrary it is the environment that makes it possible for the life of the individual to be meaningful. His thoughts, feelings and experiences as an individual are rooted in that human community to which he belongs and which is bound together in the unity of language and tradition. A nation is a community of people who share the same land, culture, language and traditions and the same awareness of a dimension of the past. The survival of a nation, it could be argued, is essential to meet the fundamental need of man, which Simone Weil speaks of as the need for roots. Hence any policy that systematically undermines the language, culture and traditions of a people inflicts a moral and intellectual injury on the nation as a whole and is a violation of Truth. It is clear then that Gandhi's nationalism, far from being unjustified, has a theological foundation; in other words it has its roots in his fundamental metaphysical beliefs concerning Truth or God. It might be argued that if Gandhi supports nationalism for the reasons suggested then he cannot rule out the possibility that the course a country might take in governing its affairs could be profoundly anti-religious. What this indicates is that religion may be a necessary condition but not a sufficient condition for the realization of nationalistic aspirations.

It might be argued also that to insist on the realization of legitimate nationalistic goals is a retrograde step, a blow to progress and a threat to internationalism. Gandhi's reply is that far from being a threat to internationalism, nationalism is in fact its prerequisite. To be an internationalist one has first to be a nationalist. Internationalism implies that people from different countries or nations come together and agree on a common policy. It is difficult to conceive of nationalism as he understands it as being a retrograde step or a blow to progress. He sought Swarāj for India not in order that she might erect barriers against other nations but rather that she might 'find full self-expression for the benefit and service of humanity at large'.[17] If it were to be objected that the proliferation of nations in the world simply leads to more problems in the form of cultural, economic and political barriers, coupled with the growth of selfishness, narrowness and exclusiveness, Gandhi's answer would be to draw a distinction between nationalism and dogmatic exclusivism, and to insist on the importance of cultural growth and development and of the need for the preservation of one's own national traditions if a sense of meaninglessness and alienation is to be avoided. In short, he would, as we have indicated, stress the need for roots. It is for this reason that he approves of patriotism. It is not a narrow, selfish or exclusive attitude as far as he is concerned. It embraces the whole of humanity and seeks the common good. It derives from religion and, therefore, is consistent with recognition of the fact that all men are brothers and with the desire to seek the welfare of all mankind. To serve one's own nation is not inconsistent with the service of humanity as a whole. Patriotism or nationalism and sarvodaya are like two sides of the same coin and not, as is generally supposed, mutually exclusive concepts. Gandhi expresses this point well when he maintains: 'My love, therefore, of nationalism or my idea of nationalism is that my country may become free, that if need be the whole of the country may die, so that the human race may live. There is no room for race hatred there. Let that be our nationalism.'[18]

When Gandhi maintains that patriotism or nationalism is derived from religion he is claiming in fact that it is essential to his understanding of Truth or God and he describes India's freedom as an expression of Truth and essential to the worship of God. This bears out what has already been said about the metaphysical presuppositions of Gandhi's nationalism and if we were to examine this point further we would need to look again at his concept of Truth and religion. The realization of Truth, as we have seen, is synonymous with the realization of the Self and the understanding of ultimate reality. This understanding of the nature of ultimate reality comes to him as a participant in the Hindu way of life. It is through the specific content or the essential teaching of his own religious tradition with its particular mode of discourse that he obtains his glimpses of Truth or God. The preservation of that form of life and mode of discourse can only be ensured ultimately by means of Swarāj, which he maintains also provides him with the possibility of full self-expression.

Gandhi's concept of religion, as we have shown, corresponds to his concept of Truth; it is what binds man to the Truth. It is belief in ṛta, or an ordered moral government of the universe; it is that permanent element in human nature that makes man seek to be at one with God. But if I am what I am because I live, move, and have my being, within a particular religious and cultural context, then that permanent element in my nature which seeks unity with Truth has to come to an understanding of Truth within that particular religious and cultural context. To put it in another way, the means of realizing Truth is bound up with patriotism; that is, nationalism like sarvodaya is related to Truth.

It is both an expression of Truth and the means of realizing it. As Gandhi states: 'I work for India's freedom because my *swadeshi* teaches me that being born in it and having inherited her culture, I am fitted to serve *her* and *she* has a prior claim to my service.'[19] It is through the service of his immediate neighbours, therefore, that Gandhi professes to come to a realization of Truth or God, but such service is not selfish or exclusive nor does it involve the exploitation of others. Rather it is consistent with the service of the whole of humanity.

If this is a correct interpretation of Gandhi's concept of Swarāj then it is possible to draw a comparison with Tillich's view of nationalism. Nationalism, for Tillich, indicates the religious content of the secular and is classified with humanism and socialism as one of the quasi-religions. It points to the need to relinquish the notion of an absolute dichotomy between the sacred and the secular. The term quasi has no pejorative connotation and simply means that nationalism has some of the characteristics one normally associates with religion. Like humanism, nationalism has a theonomous element and, according to Tillich, it is an expression of the need for self-affirmation and fills the gap that is created by a discarded religion. When it provides the consciousness of vocation, or when it gives life meaning and purpose, it partakes of the nature and shows the characteristics of a religion; it represents the ultimate principle. When it elevates itself to the level of the ultimate, however, and ignores its own finiteness, then it ceases to represent the ultimate principle and instead assumes the form of the demonic. The demonization of nationalism is Fascism and the essence of demonization here is that a preliminary concern is given the status of ultimate concern; the finiteness of the nation is ignored. The consequence of such an action is that ignoble activities, such as the suppression of criticism, the murder of opponents and systematic lying are considered justifiable activities. No appeal to a higher authority or principle is possible for the nation or state has set itself up as the ultimate principle.[20]

Gandhi regards nationalism as constituting an expression of Truth which in Tillichian terms would mean that it has some of the characteristics of religion. That is, it has a religious content and at the same time indicates that there is no absolute dichotomy between the sacred and the secular. It is consistent with acknowledging that all men are brothers, and with the desire to seek the good of all mankind. That it is capable of giving man a sense of meaning and purpose in life cannot be doubted, according to Gandhi, for he refers to it as being concerned with individual rights and ensuring even-handed justice and fair treatment to all. That it has a theonomous element is also made clear for, in Gandhi's view, it is an expression of Truth, is related to the worship of God, and seeks the welfare of humanity as a whole. Its interrelationship with sarvodaya is such that to seek Swarāj is to desire the good of all men, and it is through the service of humanity that we come to a better understanding of Truth or God.

The means for the attainment of Swarāj for Gandhi, as we have shown, are Truth and ahiṁsā. It is understandable, therefore, in view of his adherence to this basic presupposition, that he should claim not to be able to have pride in his country if she should ever attain her so-called 'freedom' by violent means.

'True democracy or the swarāj of the masses can never come through untruthful and violent means, for the simple reason that the natural corollary to their use would be to remove all opposition through the suppression or extermination of the antagonists. That does not make for individual freedom. Individual freedom can have the fullest play only under a regime of unadulterated ahimsā.'[21]

Gandhi extended his principle of Truth and non-violence to his dealings with the British government which imposed its rule on India and prevented her from governing herself. At a time when the younger intellectuals of the Congress Party were seeking or looking for action to oust the British from India, Gandhi wrote a letter to the Viceroy of India, Lord Irwin, to point out the iniquities of British rule and the precise action he proposed to take in the case of the salt tax that had been imposed on the Indian people. In that letter he referred to British rule as a curse, since among other things it impoverished millions by exploitation, made political serfs of the people and undermined the traditions and culture of India. The salt tax against which he was protesting had imposed intolerable burdens on the poor and had undermined their health in the process. He indicated the action that he proposed to take if there was no change of heart on the part of the authorities. It involved civil disobedience, though, as in every other instance of civil disobedience or non-cooperation he had engaged in, Gandhi maintained that his purpose was to persuade and convert rather than to coerce. The salt march from Sabarmati to Dandi culminated in the symbolic act of picking up grains of salt from the sea-shore. It was a direct challenge to British law which sought to preserve a Government monopoly of salt production and distribution. The flouting of the law that followed that symbolic act resulted in many thousands, including Gandhi himself, being arrested and imprisoned.[22]

If it is maintained that the salt march and the subsequent raid on the Dharasana Salt Works when scores of satyāgrahis were injured, although non-violent, nevertheless caused acute embarrassment to the British Government and could, therefore, be construed as a form of moral coercion, Gandhi would reply that it was never his intention to apply moral coercion. At the outbreak of the Second World War, for instance, he pledged not to embarrass the British Government by engaging in acts of civil disobedience unless there were grave reasons for so doing. Here he explicitly recognized that his actions could be a cause of embarrassment but he would evidently wish to draw a distinction between causing embarrassment and applying moral coercion. His pledge that if India were to be granted self-government, Britain and her allies would be permitted to retain their troops on Indian soil, is a further indication of his concern not to place the British Government in an awkward and embarrassing position.[23]

Gandhi's position on the question of whether or not moral coercion is involved in acts of civil disobedience and non-cooperation has already been referred to earlier and need not be re-examined here. What needs to be noted, however, is that in spite of everything Gandhi said about British rule in India it is clear that he still had a high regard for the British people. He claimed to have been their friend always and recalled with gratitude the kindness and hospitality he had received during his visits to England. He believed that as a people they were 'not devoid of a sense of justice' and that ultimately India would achieve her freedom non-violently.[24] It so happens that subsequent events showed his belief to be justified as far as India's dealings with the British were concerned.

Gandhi's hopes for a free India find expression in his *Hind Swaraj or Indian Home Rule*. He describes it as epitomizing the gospel of love, self-sacrifice and satyāgraha and as a repudiation of the use of force or violence. He compared the use of force for the realization of self-government to the planting of a noxious weed in the hope that it would produce a rose.[25] The assumption behind the use of force is that there is no connection between means and ends or else that the end justifies the means. Yet, in a most remarkable speech delivered at the opening ceremony of the Hindu University Central College in Benares, February 1916, in the presence of the Viceroy and leading Indian princes, dignitaries and officials, he condemned many aspects of British rule in India and maintained: 'If we are to receive self-government we shall have to take it. We shall never be granted self-government. Look at the history of the British Empire and the British nation; freedom-loving as it is, it will not be a party to give freedom to a people who will not take it themselves.'[26]

On the face of it this looks remarkably like an incitement to violence, but if it were to be interpreted that way it would be completely contrary to his views on Swarāj and diametrically opposed to his teaching concerning Truth and ahiṁsā. It is possible that what Gandhi is suggesting here is that since the Swarāj of a people is the sum total of the self-rule of individuals, the people of India should recognize that when they have learned to rule themselves they have already attained freedom for themselves and for India,[27] that is, mere transference of political power is not enough. But is this not tantamount to saying that freedom is simply an attitude of mind and is, therefore, there for the taking at any time? If this is so, does it not ignore the reality of the situation that political control would still rest in the hands of a foreign power? It may appear from what Gandhi says that he does regard freedom as an attitude of mind, and the fact that he did not consider it necessary for the realization of Swarāj that the English be expelled from India, provided they became Indianized, could be cited in support of this view.[28] But in actual fact it would be a mistake to assume that this is his position or that he ignores the reality of the political situation. His reference to the curse of British rule with its exploitation of the masses and its reduction of the people of India to political serfdom is sufficient proof, if proof be needed, that he was fully aware of reality of the Indian situation.

A further explanation of Gandhi's view that the Indian people would have to take self-government for themselves might be that, as far as he is concerned, no one can really be forced to accept slavery or serfdom. Only voluntary co-operation on the part of the people can ensure the successful government of a country. Should the people refuse to co-operate then the country becomes ungovernable. It is Gandhi's contention that India was given to the English in the first place. Originally they came to trade and were welcomed and assisted in their activities by Indians who, blinded by the sight of money, helped to enslave India. When the English employed an army to protect their commercial activities, British domination of India had in effect begun. Gandhi's point is that India had been enslaved by the voluntary acceptance of slavery by her people and would be set free by their voluntary acceptance of freedom. But India had not yet demonstrated the strength of her non-violent non-cooperation. If she had done so she would have already acquired her freedom.

'If India adopted the doctrine of love as an active part of her religion and introduced it in her politics, Swaraj would descend upon India from heaven.'[29] True Swarāj for Gandhi then is self-rule or self-control which is achieved by means of ahiṁsā and satyāgraha and through the practice of swadeshī by the people. It could never be a free gift; it had to be earned by determination

and suffering; it would be the direct result of patience, perser-
verance and courage.[30]

Gandhi's acceptance of the interrelated concepts of Truth and
ahiṁsā as fundamental to his social and political philosophy
makes it difficult if not impossible for him to approve of communism as an acceptable form of social order or as a political ideology.
He makes this point clear when he rejects its materialistic presuppositions and its defence of the use of violent methods to achieve its
ends. The materialistic goals of communism and its emphasis on
force were contrary to his professed belief in the supremacy of the
spiritual over the material and the superiority of the power of
love and non-violence to that of brute force. He regarded the
growth of state power with a great deal of misgiving because while
it removed exploitation on the one hand, it tended to undermine
individual initiative and freedom on the other. The end here,
no matter how praiseworthy it might be considered to be, did
not justify the means used to attain it. As Gandhi explains: 'I want
freedom for full expression of my personality. I must be free to
build a staircase to Sirius if I want to.'[31]

He approved of many of the motives and ideals of communism.
He regarded the communist ideal of a classless society as something
worth striving for and he agreed that the inequalities of society
were iniquitous. It was on this account that he expressed the belief
that India would be unfit for Swarāj as long as she tolerated the
fact that one fifth of the population, namely, the untouchables,
were kept in a perpetual state of bondage. He approved of the
way in which Marx sided with the poor and sought to improve
their lot and he greatly admired his industry and acumen. He also
approved of the self-sacrificing spirit and noble example of renunciation shown by many of Marx's followers, but he refused to
accept that the use of violent methods were justified in attaining
communist ideals. He recognized that the communist goal of the
abolition of the institution of private property was but another
form of the ethical ideal of non-possession or dispossession that
he himself supported in the field of economics. The difference
between the two ideals was that Gandhi advocated voluntary

acceptance of the doctrine of trusteeship, or at the most peaceful persuasion, while communism did not rule out the use of force to bring about the desired end. Gandhi makes this point clear: 'But from what I know of Bolshevism it not only does not preclude the use of force but freely sanctions it for the expropriation of private property and maintaining the collective State ownership of the same.'[32] This method was not one that Gandhi could accept, nor could he tolerate the way in which the communists, despite their denial of the charge, seemed to make a profession of trouble shooting and in the process obscured the distinction between right and wrong.

We have described Gandhi as being an advocate of a voluntary form of socialism because of his doctrine of trusteeship. Socialism is clearly a word that appeals to him since it implies a measure of equality. But should socialism be taken to imply that it would be quite in order to dispossess those who have possessions then Gandhi would repudiate it for the same reason as he repudiates communism. The socialism he favours is not acquired by cutting off the prince's head in order to make him equal to the peasant. A truly socialist society can only be established, in Gandhi's view, by truthful, non-violent means.

'Truth and *ahimsa* must incarnate in socialism. In order that they can, the votary must have a living faith in God... This God is a living Force. Our life is of that Force. That Force resides in, but is not the body. He who denies the existence of that great Force, denies to himself the use of that inexhaustible power and thus remains impotent... The socialism of such takes them nowhere...'[33] The metaphysical basis of Gandhi's political philosophy is made explicit here. His socialism, which, he claims, is a natural development of his ideas and not a philosophy that he has acquired, springs from his belief in the interrelation of Truth and ahimsā. It is a form of socialism that would never tolerate the use of force but would nevertheless sanction the use of the non-violent methods of satyāgraha in order to secure social justice. It could be argued that when Gandhi refers to the basis of socialism as economic equality he is implying, whether he realizes it or not, that some form of class struggle is inevitable and that he is thereby supporting the communist line. Yet he explicitly denies the inevitability of class conflict and maintains that when India achieved independence class antagonism would cease.

'I have no doubt whatsoever that, if non-violence in its full measure becomes the policy of the State, we shall reach essential equality without strife.'[34] Clearly Gandhi has in mind here the kind of ideal state of independence that the term Swarāj connotes, which is not simply political power or self-determination, and he would probably be the first to admit that the independence India eventually realized did not conform to the ideal he envisaged. His idea of equality, as we have shown, does not seek the elimination of capitalists but the voluntary acceptance of the doctrine of trusteeship and the establishment of right relationships between capital and labour. He bases his faith firmly on the power of ahiṁsā to achieve the economic equality that constitutes the foundation of his theory of social justice.

'I have always held that social justice, even unto the least and lowliest, is impossible of attainment by force. I have believed that it is possible by proper training of the lowliest by non-violent means to secure the redress of the wrongs suffered by them. That means is non-violent non-cooperation.'[35]

When Gandhi claims that Truth and ahiṁsā must incarnate in socialism and that he has no doubt that non-violent methods can bring it about, the question that arises is whether he is contradicting his views concerning the unattainability and non-realizability of the absolute. He stresses, as we have seen, that he has glimpses only of absolute Truth and that he has to content himself with making relative truth his beacon and guide. To claim that in the political sphere it is possible to realize the ideal through the implementation of non-violent methods could be interpreted as a form of idolatry or an example of demonization. Can any political system be regarded as an incarnation of Truth and thereby identifiable with the absolute? This is not to say that the ideal cannot determine the way in which a man thinks and acts or inspire the spirit in which he travels. Such a view would be consistent with belief in the empirical unattainability of absolute Truth and more in accord with Gandhi's basic position.

Gandhi's teaching concerning peace is a further indication of the importance he attaches to the method of non-violence and the possiblity of its implementation on a wider scale. Not to believe in the possibility of permanent peace, in his view, is to doubt the divinity or godliness of human nature.[36] Whether he has taken too optimistic a view of human nature is another question. We might be justified in interpreting this statement as an indication of an inability to recognize the frailty of human nature, or else a failure to take the reality of evil seriously. For Gandhi, however, the statement is simply an affirmation of his fundamental metaphysical belief that Truth or God, which is ultimate reality, is at one with the real Self of man. Permanent peace is possible when men know themselves, and recognize their essential unity with Truth or God, and when they realize the things that belong to their peace, such as the renunciation of imperialistic designs, territorial claims and the use of weapons of destruction. War is a reflection of man's greed and the spirit of exploitation. When these are removed the need for armaments is removed. The way of liberation from the tragedy of war is 'through a bold and unconditional acceptance of the non-violent method with all its glorious implications.'[37] Gandhi's belief in the identity of Truth and the real Self of man is reflected in his affirmation of the unity of mankind and in his professed desire to live in a united world.

We have already referred to Gandhi's attitude to war. His avowal of ahiṁsā did not prevent him, as we have seen, from participating in war in a non-combatant capacity nor from supporting a recruiting campaign. His explanation of his actions was that as a citizen of the British Empire he felt he had a duty to support it, and that he was justified in pointing out to those who did not share his attitude to war that they had a duty to fight. It may be possible to describe his attitude to non-violence as a form of casuistry.[38] He does examine each case or each situation on its merits and decides what action to take in the light of the prevailing circumstances. Violence is preferable to cowardice, for example, and fulfilling one's duty is important even if in the process it involve violence, or participation in violence in the sense of giving actual or moral support. But Gandhi's doctrine of ahiṁsā is not to be construed as an absolutist code of conduct although it has to be admitted that his condemnation of war does have an absolutist ring about it. The prevailing conditions in particular situations and the considerations of duty have to be borne in mind when determining the course of action to be taken or adopted. Such an approach makes it difficult for Gandhi to propound the doctrine of ahiṁsā as an absolutist theory of morals or a blueprint of morality to which there can be no exceptions. The principle of ahiṁsā is absolute in the sense that it informs the spirit and the circumstances in which violence is done. The relativism of his application of the concept of ahiṁsā simply corresponds to the relativism of his understanding of Truth. As perfect or absolute Truth is beyond his grasp so also is perfect or absolute ahiṁsā. He has glimpses only of absolute Truth and absolute ahiṁsā, like absolute Truth, is that which determines the way he thinks and acts and informs the spirit in which he lives. In this respect at least Gandhi is consistent and it would not be correct to suggest that he fails to see or recognize the ambivalence of his moral teaching on ahiṁsā.[39] He is prepared to acknowledge that the practice of non-violence is not possible in every situation but he can still maintain that 'the more it is practised the more effective and inexhaustible it becomes... Belief in non-violence is based on the assumption that human nature in the essence is one and therefore unfailingly responds to the advances of love...'.[40]

Gandhi's advocacy of a voluntary form of socialism as the most acceptable form of political system possible should not be taken to imply that in his view the ideal is capable of being embodied in a particular empirical form. His reference to Truth and ahimsā needing to incarnate in socialism seems to suggest such a possiblity but, on the other hand, his insistence that relative truth has to be our beacon and guide in the empirical world since we have glimpses only of absolute Truth would point to the impossibility of there being any particular empirical form of the absolute ideal. This does not mean, however, that we settle for less in the political sphere any more than we do in the economic sphere in the sense that the ideal is dispensed with or discarded. The ideal still informs the spirit in which we approach political systems in the same way as the concept of absolute Truth informs our choice of relative truths to be our guide. What Gandhi is proposing is a political system that, in his view, approximates to the ideal and is in accord with the spirit of Truth.

NOTES TO CHAPTER IX

1 *All Men are Brothers*, p. 64.
2 Ibid., p. 69.
3 *In Search of the Supreme*, Vol. 2, pp. 251–2.
4 Ibid., p. 308; cf. *All Men are Brothers*, p. 59.
5 *All Men are Brothers* p. 69.
6 *Selected Works*, Vol. VI, p. 435.
7 Ibid., pp. 438–40.
8 Ibid., p. 436.
9 Peter Winch. 'Authority and Rationality', *The Human World*, No. 8, August, 1972, pp. 9–21.
10 Op. cit., p. 14.
11 Op. cit., pp. 19–20.
12 Op. cit., p. 21.
13 *Selected Works*, Vol. VI, pp. 442–3, cf. *The Essential Gandhi*, p. 116.
14 *Selected Works*, Vol. VI, p. 445.
15 Ibid., p. 247.
16 'Responsibility to Society', *Without Answers*, (Routledge & Kegan Paul, London, 1969), pp. 86–90.
17 *Selected Works*, Vol. VI, p. 246.
18 Ibid., p. 248.
19 *All Men are Brothers*, p. 120.
20 *Christianity and the Encounter of the World Religions*, pp. 4–7 and 14–17; *Ultimate Concern*, pp. 11–12, 29, 34, 54; *Systematic Theology* Vol. 1 pp. 241–2; Vol. III, pp. 262–64.
21 *All Men are Brothers*, pp. 138–9.
22 *The Essential Gandhi*, pp. 260–2.
23 Ibid., pp. 337–9.
24 Ibid., pp. 267–8 and 340.
25 Ibid., p. 124.
26 Ibid., p. 130.
27 Ibid., p. 123; *Selected Works*, Vol. IV, p. 155.
28 *The Essential Gandhi*, p. 124.
29 *Selected Works*, Vol. IV, p. 97.
30 *Selections from Gandhi*, p. 129; *Selected Works*, Vol. IV, p. 201.
31 *Selected Works*, Vol. VI, p. 237; *The Essential Gandhi*, p. 304.
32 *Selected Works*, Vol. VI, p. 240. John E. Smith makes the same point and thereby supports Gandhi's position when he maintains that the revolutionary, Marxist or otherwise, 'who seeks to destroy an institution solely on the ground that it represents the capitalist establishment is, despite his *ultimate* ideal, nihilistic to the extent that his violence is unaccompanied by any sense of responsibility for reconstruction.' 'The inescapable ambiguity of non-violence', *Philosophy East and West*, Vol. 19, Number 2, (April 1969) pp. 155–6.

33 M. K. Gandhi, *Satyagraha*, (Ahmedabad, 1951), p. 352.
34 *Selected Works*, Vol. VI, p. 426.
35 *All Men are Brothers*, p. 138.
36 Ibid., p. 122; *Truth is God*, p. 143.
37 *All Men are Brothers*, p. 123.
38 Karl Potter, 'Explorations in Gandhi's Theory of Non-violence', *The Meanings of Gandhi*, edited by Paul F. Power, (University Press, Hawaii. 1971) pp, 91–118.
39 Paul F. Power, 'Mahatma Gandhi and Civil Disobedience', *The Meanings of Gandhi*, pp. 165–182.
40 *The Essential Gandhi*, p. 331.

CHAPTER X

CONCLUSION

Summary and Assessment

In the foregoing analysis of Gandhi's philosophy I have tried to show that certain fundamental religious and ethical beliefs acquired within Hinduism inform his teaching and determine his way of life.[1] Central to his philosphy is the concept of Truth and it is not without significance that he sub-titles his autobiography 'the story of my experiments with Truth'. It is evident that he sought to live his life in the spirit of Truth and in accordance with the religious and ethical ideals of the Hindu way of life. The early Hindu tradition refers to ultimate reality as Brahman, the substratum of existence, which in the Advaita or non-dualist tradition is identified with Ātman, the innermost Self and principle of life, and it refers to the eternal law and the moral law, which man is required to live in accordance with as the sanatana dharma and ṛta. Gandhi preserves the metaphysical and ethical connotation of these Hindu terms by his use of Satya or Truth. For him Truth is the essence of reality since nothing is except Truth and, like Brahman of the earlier tradition, Truth is Sat-Cit-Ānanda, Being Consciousness, Bliss. That he should claim to have had glimpses only of absolute Truth is understandable since, like Brahman, it is the ideal beyond predication, the neti neti, (not this, not this) which cannot be embodied in concrete particulars.

Gandhi's affirmation of Truth is a matter of faith and informs the spirit in which he lives. As the basis of all things and the substance of morality it is the *raison d'être* of his existence.[2] He is not able to encapsulate Truth in any particular form since it is always beyond man's empirical grasp, yet by holding on to such truth as he is able to apprehend in this world he understands what it means to speak of absolute Truth. It is through his participation in the Hindu way of life and his awareness of the need to live and act in accordance

with the religious and ethical ideals of Hinduism that he understands what it means to speak of Truth. His expressed preference
for the statement 'Truth is God' rather than 'God is Truth' is
explicable partly because of the different connotation of the term
Truth in the latter context. It could be maintained that it loses its
meaning as the essence of reality or the basis of all things when it is
used as a description or attribute of God.

The relation between absolute Truth and relative truth in
Gandhi's thought is paralleled by what he has to say about the
relation between Religion and religions. The former is the non-pre-
dicable ideal which cannot be embodied in finite form. No particular religion is equatable with Religion for the latter is what underlies all religions and binds man to the Truth. In Gandhi's case it is
the Hindu way of life that enables him to understand what Religion
means in the same way as relative truth enables him to understand
what it means to speak of absolute Truth. In both cases the particular conveys the meaning of the ideal. The particular does not
embody the ideal, hence no particular religion can lay claim to
a monopoly of Truth. When adherents of a particular religion
claim superiority over other religions because they believe they
possess the fullness of Truth, it could be regarded as a particularization of the absolute or a form of demonization. In Gandhi's
terminology this is equivalent to making a fetish of a religion. All
religions, in his view, are simply different roads to the same goal.
A person may choose one road rather than another; that is a personal matter. But to proselytize on the grounds of belief in the
superiority of a particular religion is to make that religion a fetish.
The greatest or over-riding need, in Gandhi's view, is for toleration, not in the sense that one is prepared to compromise one's
beliefs, but in the sense that one is prepared to respect different
belief systems. This could lead to the removal of prejudicial barriers
and to a better understanding of different faiths including one's
own.

The interrelation between Truth and ahiṁsā in Gandhi's thought
is not only implied in the sub-title of his autobiography but explicit
in the manner in which his religious and ethical ideals determine

his way of life. Since he views Truth as the substance of morality and the basis of existence rather than a concept to be analysed and investigated in the abstract, it is not surprising that relative truth should be his beacon and guide in life. It finds practical expression in the practice of ahiṁsā; but the way of non-violence is also the means whereby Truth is realized. The convertibility of means and ends in Gandhi's thought indicates that the Machiavellian doctrine of virtuous ends justifying evil means cannot possibly be accepted. To give credence to such a doctrine would imply that a rose could result from planting a noxious weed.

It would be a mistake to assume, however, that one can live one's life without ever resorting to violence. Empirical existence is such that situations arise which make violence in one form or another inevitable and unavoidable. It would be as much a mistake to make a fetish of ahiṁsā as it would to make a fetish of a particular religion. Whether we like it or not we are involved in hiṁsā by the very fact that we exist. In order to exist we must eat, and to eat involves us in the destruction of other forms of life. Furthermore there are situations of moral dilemma when it would be wrong of us not to act violently. This suggests that non-violence is not a blue-print of morality or an absolute rule of conduct which admits of no exceptions. Moral considerations can be involved when we choose to act in a violent way, but they are moral considerations which are related to the perspective of the action. When we act violently it does not neccesarily mean that the ideal of non-violence has been abandoned. The ahiṁsā ideal is still absolute in the sense that it informs the spirit in which violence is done. Of course, in situations of moral dilemma different considerations might apply for different people. One person might justify participation in war, for example, while another would oppose it. Gandhi would be among those totally opposed to war, yet he would not seek to prevent those who saw a justification for war from participating in it. Indeed he would be prepared to encourage them to act according to their beliefs and to do what they conceived to be their duty. This does not mean that he is abandoning his commitment to the ideal or principle of ahiṁsā; rather it is a recognition on his part that life 'is not a single straight line' governed by one general principle which can be applied in all circumstances without exceptions.

What has been said about ahiṁsā as an ideal informing the spirit in which we live and act applies equally to satyāgraha as the technique of ahiṁsā or the method of holding on to Truth. Its main purpose is conversion rather than coercion. It seeks to redress the wrongs of society and establish social justice by the power of love and gentle persuasion. Its methods might involve civil disobedience or non-cooperation, but they would be combined with persuasive reasoning and voluntary suffering and seek to promote the good of all even the good of a wrong doer. Despite Gandhi's statements to the contrary, however, a measure of coercion is involved in satyāgraha campaigns. Moral pressure is clearly brought to bear on authorities by means of satyāgraha techniques and it is not less coercive for being moral and non-violent. The problems referred to in relation to ahiṁsā, therefore, apply equally to satyāgraha. It could also be maintained that there is no abandonment of the ideal of persuasion and conversion in any of the satyāgraha campaigns, but that in certain situations actions resulting in moral pressure were determined by moral considerations involved in the perspective of the action. Gandhi was aware, for example, that his fasts, which were directed at boosting the morale of striking satyāgrahi by identifying himself with their suffering, had the additional effect of forcing his opponents into negotiation. In spite of this he still felt he had acted correctly in the circumstances. That is, the principles of love and persuasion still informed the spirit of his fasts even though they resulted in a measure of moral coercion.

Gandhi's equation of Satya, Truth and Sat, Being, with Ātman, the highest Self, which all men share, implies that the concept of sarvodaya, the welfare of all men, is a natural corrollary of Truth. Injury or hiṁsā cannot be inflicted on a fellow human being without undermining Truth. But it is not just the brotherhood of man, if one can put it that way, that is brought to the fore here but also the unitary nature of all existence. Cow worship simply epitomises

belief in the essential unity of life and the fact that though we have
many and different bodily forms we have but one soul and share
the same Ātman. Respect for all forms of life is the ideal that derives from basic presuppositions concerning the isomorphism of
Truth, Being and Self, but Gandhi recognizes that in particular circumstances one has to destroy some forms of life, such as rats
and snakes, in order to protect the lives of others. Faith in the
ideal of ahiṁsā is not shaken by such actions which on the face of
it seem to a violation of the ideal. The ideal or principle of ahiṁsā
remains inviolate in the sense that it informs the spirit in which a
man performs all his actions. This faith is illustrated in Gandhi's
rejection of utilitarianism as a moral ideal and the aim of life. In
comparison with sarvodaya it is an attenuated moral ideal and indicative of a readiness to settle for second best. Eudaemonistic
consequentialism, as Bernard Williams calls it, can hardly compete
with sarvodaya as an ideal, though advocates of utilitarianism
might well argue that it is a more realistic goal. Gandhi's acceptance
of sarvodaya, however, is not based on a realistic appraisal of what
might or might not be attainable in this life but on the metaphysical presuppositions we have referred to. His claim to see God
through the service of his fellow men is in accord with the religious
and ethical ideals characteristic of the teaching of the Gītā which
seeks renunciation *in* action rather than renunciation *of* action.

The metaphysical presupposition of the unity of existence involves him in an inescapable moral obligation to his fellow men
and shows clearly the interrelation of morality and religion in his
thought. This has far-reaching social implications which are clearly
revealed in his concern for the status of Harijans and women in
Indian society. He relinquishes his advocacy of the functional
distinctions of varṇāśramadharma in order to proclaim unequi-
vocally the need for the abolition of the caste system which, in his
view, was harmful to the moral and spiritual growth of the nation,
a blot on Hinduism, and contrary to the Truth. Nothing short of
a restoration of the purity of the Hindu way of life would suffice
to effect the social changes required to improve the lot of the outcastes. The same is true of women whose status in Indian society

because of such customs as child marriages, enforced widowhood, and purdah, was not an enviable one. The inner change and return to the religious ethical ideals of the Hindu way of life that Gandhi is advocating, however, is not meant in any pietistic sense. It is not an individualistic affair having no social implications. His metaphysical presuppositions do not permit the abdication of social responsibility or a denial of his moral obligations to his fellow men. Social changes are the necessary if not the sufficient conditions for the amelioration of the lot of both women and outcastes in Indian society and one of the means for the achievement of this end is a system of education that seeks the well-being of all the people of India. Gandhi would be the first to acknowledge that the ideal social order is not capable of being realized within the empirical realm, but that did not mean the ideal should not inform his attitude to particular social structures. His indictment of the British educational system was that it undermined the fabric of the nation by ignoring its languages and neglecting its cultural heritage. It cut at the very roots of Indian life and was a violation of Truth. His proposal for an alternative educational system may not have been ideal, but it was in harmony with the religious and ethical ideals of the Hindu way of life and, in his view, more in accord with the needs of the people of India.

If the ideal or Euclidian model is not realizable in the social sphere the same is true in the field of economics. What Gandhi seeks is an approximation to the ideal in the same way as he holds on to relative truth in the empirical realm since absolute Truth is beyond his grasp. Basically his economic policy, like that of E. F. Schumacher, is people-oriented. It reflects his quest for Truth. It rejects those economic developments that dehumanize and degrade people's lives and is an affront to their moral well-being. It encourages equitable distribution of the wealth of a nation and a recognition of the dignity of labour. Gandhi points to the dangers of an uncritical acceptance of industrialization especially the kind that amasses fortunes for the few at the expense of the many. On the other hand, he recognizes the value of the kind of industrialization that alleviates poverty, idleness and misery. The economic policy he advocates is one that preserves ethical standards and promotes the welfare and moral well-being of the nation.

If Gandhi's metaphysical presuppositions have social and economic implications, they also have political consequences. His concern for the welfare of all men means that he cannot ignore those activities that directly affect the lives of individuals. This is the reason why he refuses to draw a demarcation line between religion and politics and, as we have seen, religion for him is that which binds man to Truth. Because of his involvement in politics he has been described as one who allowed his political instincts to determine his decisions and actions. This is a misleading description and one that Gandhi rejects. Equally misleading is the claim that he is 'a political moralist who wrote from the standpoint of the rebel, who did not concern himself with the ethical and practical problems facing men in authority'.[3] His concern for the welfare of all men does not exclude men in authority and the problems they face, which was a basic reason why during satyāgraha campaigns he sought not victory over his opponents but solutions that were mutually acceptable.

The political goal of Swarāj, or self-rule, was for Gandhi grounded in Truth and the undisputed right of the people of India. But if we were to inquire of him whether any political system could embody the concepts of Truth and non-violence he would have to reply that the absolute is incapable of being incarnated in any finite empirical form. Communism falls short of the ideal because it advocates violence to achieve its ends. Gandhi seems to suggest, however, that a voluntary form of socialism might embody Truth and ahiṁsā, yet it would be more consistent with his stress on the non-realizability of the absolute in the empirical realm to maintain that what he is proposing is a political system that approximates to the ideal.

I have endeavoured to show in this work the interrelation of the concepts of Truth, ahiṁsā, satyāgraha and sarvodaya in Gandhi's thought and the way in which fundamental metaphysical beliefs acquired within the Hindu way of life inform his teaching and determine the spirit in which he lives.

Ācārya Kripalani, a close friend and follower of Gandhi, made this comment about the Mahātma at the close of our discussion in Madras: 'He wasn't a saint, you know'. Gandhi would entirely agree: in his view the term was too sacred to be applied to a simple seeker after Truth. But who can doubt that he was a most remarkable man.

NOTES TO CHAPTER X

1   I differ fundamentally from the view expressed by Joan V. Bondurant
    who states that the dialectic implicit in Gandhi's method of satyāgraha
    is not dependent on his metaphysical assumptions nor on his Hindu-based
    theology, and that his criteria of truth, like those of Marx, lie in the
    meeting of human need. See *Conquest of Violence: The Gandhian Philo-
    sophy of Conflict*, (University of California Press, 1971) pp. 192–3.
2   M. K. Gandhi, *An Autobiography*, (London, 1372), p. 29.
3   Raghavan Iyer, *The Moral and Political Thought of Mahatma Gandhi*,
    (New York, 1978), p. 374.

GLOSSARY

abhyāsa: single-minded devotion

Ācārya: a spiritual guide or teacher

adhyāsa: illegitimate transference; related to superimposition

Advaita: non-dualism; philosophical system expounded by Gaudapada and Śankara

āgraha: to hold fast; firmess of grasp

ahamkāra: ego

ahimsā: non-violence; non-injury

Ahuramazda: God of light in Zoroastrianism

ānanda: bliss; pure joy

anekāntavādin: one who maintains the non-unitary nature of reality

anicca: impermanence

aparigraha: not holding on to possessions

artha: wealth; well-being

Āryan: noble; lord; name assumed by or applied to fair-skinned nomads who migrated to India

āryavarṇa: noble; fair-skinned

āśrama: orders or stages of life; abode of holy men

ātman: highest Self; essence of life

avidyā: ignorance; lack of true knowledge

Bhagavad Gītā: Song of the Lord; literary classic of Hinduism

bhakti: devotion; worship

Brahmā: creator God; member of the Hindu triad (trimūrti)

Brahman: ultimate reality; substratum of existence

brāhman, brāhmin: member of highest caste

brahmacārya: one of four stages of life; conduct conducive to knowledge of Brahman

Buddha: the Enlightened One

buddhi: intellect; power of discrimination

cit: consciousness

charkhā: spinning-wheel

darśana: view; especially the six orthodox philosphical systems of Hinduism

dāsa varṇa: dark-coloured; dark-skinned

deva: deity

dharma: duty; law

duḥkha: suffering

Dvaita: dualism; philosophical system expounded by Madhva (12th century)

ekāntavādin: one who maintains the unitary nature of reality
gṛhastha: one of the four stages of life; householder
Harijans: Children of God; outcastes
hiṁsā: violence; injury
Īśvara: Lord
Jains: adherents of Jainism, one of three heterodox Indian systems
jāti: birth
jivan mukti: liberated soul; self-liberation
jñāna: knowledge
kāma: love; desire
karma: act, action; ethical doctrine related to consequences of actions
khādī: home-produced cloth
Kṛṣṇa: avatar or incarnation of Viṣṇu
Kṣatriyas: members of warrior caste
Mahātma: Great soul
māyā: appaerance; illusion
Mokṣa: liberation
neti neti: not this, not this
nirguṇa: without qualities
nirvāṇa: state of extinction of tānhā; craving or desire
prakṛti: nature
pūrṇa: total; complete
Rāma: avatar or incarnation of Viṣṇu
Rāmānuja: Expounder of the Viśiṣṭādvaita philosophical system (10th century)
rājanya: warrior
rāja: royal
rajas: attachment
ṛta: cosmic moral law
saccidānanda: being, consciousness, bliss; related to Brahman
sadāgraha: holding firm to reality; firmness in good cause
sadāvrata: donation; gift
śakti: power; energy
samādhi: concentrated thought; state of complete meditation
saṁsāra: bondage of birth, life, death, and rebirth; empirical existence
sanātana: eternal
sangha: order; fellowship (of Buddhists); group
Śankara: Expounder of Advaita Vedānta philosophical system (8th century)
saṁnyāsa: ascetic; stage of life
saṁnyāsin: religious mendicant, one who has relinquished worldly attachments
sarvodaya: welfare of all; universal uplift

sat: being; reality; good; true

satya: truth

satyāgraha: holding fast to truth; truth force; technique of ahiṁsā

satyāgrahi: one who adheres to principles of satyāgraha

Śiva: destroyer god, member of the Hindu triad

svadharma: one's own duty

swadeshī: self-reliance (reliance on one's country's resources)

swarāj: self-government; self-rule

Śūdra: labourer; members of the lower caste of Hinduism

syādvāda: belief in the doctrine of the many-sidedness of reality; Jain doctrine of relativism

tānhā: craving for existence; desire

tapas: austerites; warmth, heat; purificatory action

tat tvam asi: that thou art

trimūrti: Hindu triad or trinity

Upaniṣads: esoteric teaching of philosophical nature; Hindu classic

vairāgya: indifference to worldly life

Vaiśyas: Artisans; members of one of the main castes of Hinduism

vanaprastha: one of four stages of life

vānaprasthin: forest dweller

varṇa: colour; function

Vedānta: end of the Veda; one of the six orthodox Hindu philosophical systems

Vedas: four collections (samhitas) of sacred knowledge

Viśiṣṭādvaita: non-dualism with distinctions; philosophical system expounded by Rāmānuja (10th century)

Viṣṇu: preserver God; member of Hindu triad (trimūrti)

yoga: yoke; discipline

yogin: one who accepts spiritual discipline

BIBLIOGRAPHY

Haridas Bhattacharya (ed.), *The Cultural Heritage of India*, Vol. IV, The Ramakrishna Mission, Calcutta 1956.

Wm. Theodore de Bary (ed.), *Sources of Indian Tradition*, Columbia University Press, New York, 1958, Vols. I & II.

Joan V. Bondurant, *Conquest of Violence: The Gandhian Philosophy of Conflict*. University of California Press, 1965.

Nirmal Kumar Bose, *Lectures on Gandhism*, Navajivan Publishing House, Ahmedabad, 1971.

—— *Selections from Gandhi*, Navajivan Publishing House, Ahmedabad, 1948.

—— *Studies in Gandhism*, Navajivan Publishing House, Ahmedabad, 1972.

John V. Canfield, 'Wittgenstein and Zen', *Philosophy*, Vol. 50, No. 194, October, 1975.

S. N. Dasgupta, *Hindu Mysticism*, Frederick Ungar, New York, 1973.

—— *A History of Indian Philosophy*, Vols. I—V, Cambridge University Press, 1922–55.

Dhirendra Mohan Datta, *The Philosophy of Mahatma Gandhi*, University of Wisconsin Press, Madison, 1953.

Mahadev Desai, *The Gospel of Selfless Action or the Gita according to Gandhi*, Ahmedabad, 1956.

Paul Deussen, *The Philosophy of the Upanishads*, Dover Publications, New York, 1966.

Charles Eliot, *Hinduism and Buddhism*, Vols. 1-3, Routledge and Kegan Paul, London, 1954.

Dorothy Emett, 'The Ground of Being', *Journal of Theological Studies*, 1964.

Erik H. Erikson, *Gandhi's Truth*, Faber and Faber, London, 1970.

Louis Fischer, Editor, *The Essential Gandhi*, Vintage Books, New York, 1962.

M. K. Gandhi, *All Men Are Brothers*, compiled and edited by Krishna Kripalani, Unesco, 1958, and 1969.

—— *An Autobiography*, translated from Gujarati by Mahadev Desai, Jonatham Cape, London, 1972.

—— *Caste Must Go, the Sin of Untouchability*, Navajivan Publishing House, Ahmedabad, 1964.

—— *Discourses on the Gita*, Navajivan Publishing House, Ahmedabad, 1960.

—— *Ethical Religion*, Ahmedabad, 1969.

—— *Fasting in Satyagraha, its use and abuse*, Ahmedabad, 1965.

—— *For Workers against Untouchability*, Ahmedabad, 1960.

—— *In Search of the Supreme*, Vols. 1-3, compiled by V. B. Kher, Navajivan Publishing House, Ahmedabad, 1931.

—— *Non-violence in Peace and War*, 2 vols, Ahmedabad, 1960–2.

—— *Non-violent Way to World Peace*, Ahmedabad, 1959.

—— *Prayer*, compiled and edited by Chandrakant Kaji, Navajivan Publishing House, Ahmedabad, 1977.

—— *Satyagraha, Non-violent resistance*, Ahmedabad, 1951 and 1958.

—— *The Collected Works of Mahatma Gandhi*, The Publication Division, Government of India, 1958–; Vols. 1–70. Int, Publications Service.

—— *The Selected Works of Mahatma Gandhi*, Vols. 1–6, general editor, Shriman Narayan, Ahmedabad, 1968.

—— *To Students*, edited by Bharatan Kumarappa, Ahmedabad, 1953.

—— *Truth is God*, compiled by R. K. Prabhu, Ahmedabad, 1955 and 1969.

Gandhian Outlook & Techniques, Ministry of Education, Government of India, Delhi, 1953.

B. N. Ganguli, *Gandhi's Social Philosophy: Perspective and Relevance*, Vikas Publishing House, Delhi 1973.

Vinit Haksar, 'Coercive Proposals', *Political Theory*, Vol. 4, No. 1, February, 1976.

—— 'Rawl and Gandhi on Civil Disobedience', *Inquiry*, Vol. 19, No. 2, 1976.

John Hick, *The Myth of God Incarnate*, S.C.M. Press, London, 1977

M. Hiriyanna, *Outlines of Indian Philosophy*, George Allen & Unwin, Bombay 1973.

—— *The Essentials of Indian Philosophy*, George Allen & Unwin, Bombay, 1973.

Aldous Huxley, *Ends and Means*, Chatto & Windus, London 1941.

Raghavan Iyer, *The Moral and Political Thought of Mahatma Gandhi*, Oxford University Press, New York, 1973.

J. R. Jones, 'How do I know who I am', *Aristotelian Society*, Vol. XLI, 1967.

J. B. Kripalani, *Gandhi His Life and Thought*, Publications Division, Ministry of Information and Broadcasting, Government of India, New Delhi, 1970.

—— *Gandhian Thought*, Gandhi Smarak Nidhi, New Delhi, 1961.

Arend Th. Van Leeuwen, *Christianity in World History*, Edinburgh House Press, 1964.

Martin Deming Lewis (ed.), *Gandhi Maker of Modern India?* in *Problems in Asian Civilization* series, D. C. Heath and Company, Boston, 1965.

V. S. Naravane, *Modern Indian Thought*, Asia Publishing House, Bombay, 1964.

R. Otto, *Mysticism East and West*, Macmillan, New York, 1972.

D. Z. Phillips, *Faith and Philosophical Enquiry*, Routledge & Kegan Paul, London, 1970.

—— *Some Limits to Moral Endeavour*, University College of Swansea, 1971.

—— *The Concept of Prayer*, Routledge & Kegan Paul, London, 1965.

Paul F. Power (ed.), *The Meanings of Gandhi*, University Press, Hawaii, 1971.

N. Pyarelal, *Mahatma Gandhi, The Last Phase*, 2 vols., Navajivan Publishing House, Ahmedabad, 1956–7.

Sarvepalli Radhakrishnan and Charles A. Moore, *A Source Book in Indian Philosophy*, Princeton University Press, New Jersey, 1973.

S. Radhakrishnan, *Eastern Religion & Western Thought*, Oxford University Press, London, 1940.

—— *Indian Philosophy*, 2 vols., George Allen & Unwin, London, 1923–27.

S. Radhakrishnan and others, *History of Philosophy Eastern and Western*, 2 vols., George Allen & Unwin, London, 1952, 1953.

G. Ramachandran and T. R. Mahadevan, *Gandhi, his relevance for our times,* Revised edition, World without War Council, 1971.

P. Nagaraja Rao, *Contemporary Indian Philosophy,* Bharatiya Vidya Bhavan, Bombay, 1970.

Rush Rees, *Without Answers,* Routledge and Kegan Paul, London, 1969.

Glyn Richards, 'Conceptions of the Self in Wittgenstein, Hume and Buddhism: a comparison and analysis', *The Monist,* January, 1978, Vol. 61, No. 1.

S. K. Saxena, 'The Fabric of Self Suffering in Gandhi', *Religious Studies,* 12 June, 1976, Cambridge University Press.

E. F. Schumacher, *Small is Beautiful,* Harper & Row, New York, 1973.

Chandrashankar Shukla, *Gandhi's View of Life,* Bharatiya Vidya Bhavan, Bombay, 1956.

I. C. Sharma, *Ethical Philosophes of India,* revised and edited by S. M. Dauger, Harper & Row, 1970.

J. J. C. Smart and Bernard Williams, *Utilitarianism for and against,* Cambridge, 1973.

Ninian Smart, *Doctrine and Argument in Indian Philosophy,* George Allen & Unwin, London 1964.

John E. Smith, 'The inescapable ambiguity of non-violence', *Philosophy East and West,* Vol. 19, No. 2, University of Hawaii, April 1969.

D. G. Tendulkar, *Mahatma, Life of Mohandas Karamchand Gandhi,* Vols. 1–8, Vithalbhai K. Jhaveri, Bombay 1951–4; Delhi 1960–3.

The Encyclopedia of Philosophy, Vols. 1–8, Macmillan, New York, 1967.

Paul Tillich, *Christianity and the Encounter of the World Religions,* Columbia University Press, New York, 1963.

—— *Dynamics of Faith,* Harper & Row, New York, 1958.

—— *Systematic Theology,* Vols. 1–3, Nisbet, London 1968.

—— *The Courage to Be,* Nisbet, London, 1952.

—— *The Future of Religions,* edited by Jerald C. Brauer, Harper & Row, New York, 1966.

—— *The Shaking of the Foundations,* Pelican, London, 1962.

—— *Ultimate Concern: Tillich in Dialogue,* Harper & Row, New York, 1965.

Leo Tolstoy, *The Kingdom of God and Peace Essays,* Oxford University Press, 1974.

Raymond Vanover (ed.), *Eastern Mysticism,* Vol. 1, Mentor, New American Library, New York, 1977.

Surendra Verma, *Metaphysical Foundation of Mahatma Gandhi's Thought,* Orient Longmans, New Delhi, 1970.

Simone Weil, *Letter to a Priest,* London, 1953.

Peter Winch, 'Authority and Rationality', *The Human World,* No. 8, August 1972.

—— 'Understanding a Primitive Society', *Religion and Understanding.* Oxford, 1967.

Ludwig Wittgenstein, *Philosophical Investigations,* Basil Blackwell, Oxford, 1976.

—— *The Blue and Brown Books,* Blackwell, Oxford, 1958.

George Woodcock, *Gandhi,* Fontana, London, 1972.

Wm. Wordsworth, *Poetical Works*, edited by Thomas Hutchinson, Oxford University Press, 1973.

R. C. Zaehner, *Hinduism*, Oxford University Press, 1962.

—— *Hindu and Muslim Mysticism*, Schocken Books, New York, 1969.

Heinrich Zimmer, *Philosophies of India*, Bollingen Series XXVI, Princeton, New Jersey, 1951.

INDEX

abhyāsa, 10
Absolute, 2, 11, 12
action, 8, 13, 14, 38, 42, 45, 48, 49,
   52f., 71f., 80, 145, 152, 159, 160,
   161
Advaita, 1–3, 11, 13, 33, 64, 157
agape, 68–69
ahiṁsā, 9, 14, 25, 40f., 53, 56, 58,
   60f., 77, 78, 87, 88, 91, 114–116,
   120, 131, 145, 159, 160–163
   and Truth, 8, 31f., 69, 80, 81, 104,
   149, 158, 163
   and satyāgraha, 48f., 64, 68, 81,
   148, 160
   and women, 90
   and sadāvrata, 116f.
   and swarāj, 139f.
   and civil disobedience, 52, 53,
   145f.
   and communism, 149f., 163
   and socialism, 150f., 163
   and war, 152f., 159
Ahmedabad, 54, 61
Ahuramazda, 4
Allah, 14
Ambedkar, 85
American, 106
ānanda, 1, 157
Anekāntavādin, 3
anger, 33, 34, 41, 50, 60, 97
anicca, 126
aparigraha, 55
artha, 57
Aryan, 81–2
ascetic, 56, 57, 75
āśrama, 56f., 81f.
atheism, 2, 77
Ātman, 11, 49, 64, 69, 75, 95, 104,
   109, 112, 157, 160, 161
   and Truth, 13, 32f., 64, 121, 143,
   152

and Brahman, 13
atom bomb, 43
austerities, 75
autobiography, 1, 92, 157, 158
avidyā, 13, 69

Banaras, 5, 147
beacon, 11, 34, 86, 110, 151, 153, 159
Being, 1, 2, 4, 7, 157, 161
Bettiah, 35
Bhagavad Gītā, 5, 8, 14, 24, 33, 41,
   75, 82, 116, 121, 161
bhakti, 13
Bible, 5, 14, 24, 116
birth (jāti), 8, 57, 75, 82, 84, 85, 86
   109
birth control, 59, 92, 94
bishops, 25
bliss, 1
blunders, 11
Bolshevism, 150
Bondaref, T.M., 116
Bourke-White, M., 43
boycott, 120
Brahma, 7
brahmacārya, 56f., 92, 108, 136
Brahman, 4, 11, 13, 81, 92, 157
Brāhman, 81f., 108, 116
bread labour, 116–7
British, 45, 60, 105, 106, 109, 120,
   141f., 152, 162
brotherhood, 20, 78, 135, 160
buckler, 11
Buddha, 24, 26, 69
Buddhism, Buddhists, 2, 67f., 75,
   126, 127

Calcutta, 116
Calvinistic, 58